LIVING [illegible]

THE AN[illegible]

By

Stephen Thornton

ISBN: 979-8-9891458-2-9

Acknowledgement

Thank you to all my friends, who inspired me to write this book. Special thanks go to Leanne Walker, who gave me the firm belief I could do it. Also Lesley George who kept me going, even though it was hard sometimes, and putting up with me. For everyone who gave me hope and encouraged me to keep writing.

Thank you, Josie, Sofia, Sarah and Mary, for your assistance.

Thank you, the reader for buying this book.

IF I CAN DO IT, SO CAN YOU!

About the Author

Stephen was born in London and is currently living in South Wales, after residing in several locations within the British isles.

When he is not writing, or working for Spirit, his hobbies include reading, (especially science fiction) and baking. His signature bake is Lemon Drizzle Cake.

Table of Contents

Chapter 1

Being Different

The first thing I learned was that I was not like other children.

Mum told me that when she put me in a playpen, as a baby, I would just sit there doing nothing; I ignored the toys and stared into open space like I was in my own world. I made no attempt to crawl, and I never put food in my mouth until I was 18 months old. As a newborn, the doctors did not expect me to live. The staff would give me the last rites every evening before they went off duty. They were shocked to find me still alive in the morning. I was such a small baby; I was placed in an incubator for three weeks. I was fed intravenously, and they dressed me in doll clothes. I had a cawl on my face, a second layer of skin; old wives' tales said this meant I would never drown. If sailors had a bottle with a cawl in on the ship, it was said it would never sink. Apparently, it was worth a lot of money as it was very rare for a baby to be born with this. "The jar the nurses placed it in was stolen from the hospital," Dad told me one day. "It was valued at £50." Dad did the football; on the Thursday I was born, he won for the first and only time, one hundred pounds. Because I was so ill, once I came out of the hospital, he took Mum, sister Susan, and me on a holiday.

It seemed I was always in and out of the doctors. Whether it was for a sore throat, which I suffered with quite a lot, or a headache. Often, my Mum would take me on a bus and then an underground train to a large hospital in London, where I was born. There, the doctors would check my reflexes. One young lady doctor, who I liked, used to make me laugh. Her name was Margaret Smelly. She was very pretty; long, dark brown straight hair tied, so it was neat and tidy. I remember being weighed and then measured to see how tall I was.

"Can you walk across the room for me?" Doctor Smelly asked me. I looked at my Mum, and when she nodded her head, I walked across the room. The doctor wrote notes in her book. "Now, let me see if you can hop on your right foot." I tried hopping, which was quite easy. "Good, now can you hop on the other foot?" she smiled with appreciation. I hopped and fell over. "Oh my," Doctor Smelly picked me up and asked me to try again. I tried hopping, but I lost my balance. "Never mind, nothing to worry about," the doctor said. "Stephen seems to have come along very well." Speaking to my Mum, "I would like to see Stephen in another six months." After we made the appointment, we left.

Other visits to the hospital were for different reasons; I saw some doctors about my eyes. I had a pronounced squint in my left eye, which was noticeable to everyone who saw me. My left eye looked way out, rather than the usual squint where the eye turned inwards. Another time, my Mum took me up to London to see another doctor somewhere else in the huge hospital. I remember walking down our road, with Mum holding my hand, to a busier street.

We lived on a large council estate where all the streets were named after composers. We lived in Sullivan Way, in a semi-detached three-bedroomed house with two downstairs rooms - a dining room and a lounge. The kitchen had a back door on the side of the house, leading to a porch facing the next-door neighbour's back door. The porch was dark, with an outside disused toilet and two bunkers for coal and coke, for the fires and stove. In those days, central heating was not heard of. The road we lived in went through the middle of the estate, and all the other streets led off of it.

At the end of our street was the main road where the bus stopped. "Be careful, Stephen, hold my hand tightly as we cross the road," Mum said cheerfully. I held on for dear life. A short while later, the bus came along. It was not a long ride to the train station. I looked out of the window, watching the scenery go by. Fields of horses, then a huge roundabout (which the bus went straight over) up a steep hill, past another hospital at the top on the left. "That is the orthopedic hospital," my Mum explained.

"What is an ortho…?" I could not say word.

"If you broke a bone, like if you fell over and broke your arm or leg, you would go to that hospital to get better." My Mum replied. Later, when I was nine years old, I spent a whole month in that orthopedic hospital.

In my mind, I had the prettiest mother in the world. She was not too tall, although, being just a child, she seemed as tall as a house. Dark brown curly hair, hazel eyes, and a slim figure, despite having us children. Mum always wore high heels when she went out. Dressed smartly in a nice flowery dress, she wore pink lipstick. I used to see her putting a blusher on her cheeks.

We finally arrived at the railway station. Stanmore Underground and Mum bought the tickets. "One and a half return to Warren Street," she would say. The ticket man would tell Mum what the price was, then tear off a ticket. Down some steps we would go, me holding Mum's hand, to where several tiny red trains stood at different platforms. "We need platform 2," Mum said. "Can you see a number two?" Mum asked me. I looked around but could not see the numbers because everything far away was a blur.

We sat in the train. There was hardly anyone else there, so we had a choice of which carriage to sit in. Mum often chose the sixth carriage; there seemed to be so many. A few minutes later, the train began to move; it seemed to go really fast. "How come this train does not make any noise?" I asked, and Mum laughed.

The doctor, this time, was a very softly-spoken middle-aged man. He wore a dark suit rather than a white coat. He was clean-shaven with neatly combed black hair; I liked his colourful tie. Mum sat me on a separate chair while the doctor spoke to her. She answered him and had a worried look on her face. Then suddenly, he turned to me. "How are you, Stephen?" he asked. He had a big smile on his face. I had no idea what to say. He asked me to follow his finger and copy, with my finger, what he did. "Touch your nose with your left finger, like I am doing." I copied him. After a few more exercises, he frowned and wrote some notes in a folder. "There seems to be something not quite right." He then spoke to my Mum about things that I did not understand. "Come back and see me in four months." When we arrived home, Mum gave me some sweets for being a good boy. On later visits to see that doctor, I found out his name was Doctor Soddy.

I had two siblings: an older sister, Susan, and a younger brother, John. Susan was 18 months older than me, and John was 14 months younger. They were both able to do things that I found difficult, like catching a ball, balancing on one leg, or doing handstands. Though I tried, I lost my balance and often cried because I felt so frustrated with myself.

When we had visitors, whether it be my parents' friends or relatives, I seemed to be singled out for unwanted attention. By this, I mean they used to talk about what I could do, which did not appear to be much. Apparently, I never crawled like other babies. I did not put things in my mouth like other kids. I felt that they all were all feeling sorry for me. They used to sit there and say things like, "Can Stephen do this yet?" and "Is he able to run properly?" "Oh, he has a funny squint in his eye. Poor little boy." It was years later, when I was nine years old, that I learned the truth about why I was always attending hospital appointments.

It seemed most people looked at me as a child with difficulties. The word 'Spastic' was used in those days. If I managed to achieve something, everyone clapped; it was almost like they believed I was not able to do anything. I was quite clumsy; I often dropped things and then struggled to pick them up, compared to my brother John. Often, people would take us as twins as we wore similar clothes and looked very alike, there being only 14 months between us.

I appeared to struggle with everything; I was not able to see the television unless I sat right in front of it. Being labeled as a child with difficulties was something I had to deal with. I began to realize how different things were when I was four years old.

Chapter 2

Tom

When I was four, things began to change. I felt someone was watching over me, though I could not understand who it might be.

We had a log fire in our sitting room, and because I was always sitting on the floor watching the television, I often watched the flames dance as the logs burned. Dad put a grate in front of the fire so we did not get too close. Staring into the flames, I was sure I could see people in there: a man in a suit wearing a bowler hat. A woman walking through with a bag full of shopping or clothes. Sometimes, a crowd of people just sit in the fire reading or playing games. When I first saw these people, I could not understand why the rest of my family could not see them, too.

"Look, Mum, can you see the people in the fire?" I asked. Everyone stopped and looked at the burning logs. "You must have a good imagination," Dad remarked. "I cannot see anything." Neither could anyone else. I looked into the flames again. There was nobody there. "Come away from the fire," Mum said. "You are sitting too close." I shuffled away and focused on the television.

Sometimes, if it was cold, Mum would light a fire during the day. As I said earlier, we did not have any central heating back then, but Dad had paraffin burners, which we had used occasionally. When the fire was well-lit, Susan and John would sit there giggling. "Can you see anything in the fire?" they would ask. Sometimes, before I could open reply, John would sit forward and exclaim, "Look, Susan, I can see a doggy running, and.... Ooh, an elephant, too." He would point to the fire. Susan peered into the flames. "Umm, not too sure." I had a feeling John was making it up.

"Well, Stephen, you can see the elephant and doggy, can't you?" he asked.

I was not sure what to say. I focused on the flames. Nothing! John laughed, but Susan tried not to. I had the feeling Susan was trying to be nice to me. At last, John owned up; he had not seen an elephant or a doggy in the flames.

Susan stood up and walked over to me. "I know you are a special brother, "she put her arms around me and gave me a cuddle."I believe you," she whispered. I almost cried with joy. Someone actually believed I could see things. I had often wondered if it was just my imagination.

Was it my imagination? I thought about that in bed later. I slept in the front room in a double bed I shared with John. It was the box room, just big enough for a double bed, a set of drawers, and a few toys.

When I fell asleep, I had bad dreams*; I was being chased by animals from the Zoo - lions, cheetahs, tigers, and all sorts. As I ran, I felt anxious; I knew if these animals* *caught me, they would tear me to shreds and eat me up. I noticed alongside me were penguins, rabbits, and guinea pigs - all running away from the animals behind us. I glanced around; they were slowly catching up with us. We ran faster; we all felt terrified. I ran and ran; the penguins and others all encouraged me to get home before they caught us. Through the streets, we ran. Still, the lions and cheetahs, joined now by elephants and panthers, chased us, roaring and snarling in our wake. It was getting dark now, and the fear of being killed was immense. Frightened out of my wits, I turned a corner, taking another look to see how far behind they were. Oh my! They were so close; I could smell their breath. With a joyous roar, the lion and panther pounced.*

I woke up in my bed, under the blankets, shaking and sweating. The dream seemed to fade, but the detail was clear. It was a bad nightmare. I kept having this nightmare, and others like it, for the next ten years.

In another nightmare, I was trying to get home; *behind me was a double-decker bus full of people. I had a feeling these people, if they caught up with me, would kill me. I ran as fast as I could. I reached the road where I lived, anxious to get home before the bus caught me. I heard the engine as the bus slowly caught up with me. It was so close. I ran faster and turned into my front garden, slamming the gate behind me. I was terrified now, as the bus was right behind me. I could see the faces of the people on the top deck scowling at me. Felt the overwhelming need to get upstairs into the safety of my bed, where I would be safe; I pushed the front door open and rushed up the stairs, two at a time, panting, almost out of breath. Running into my bedroom, I saw the decker bus outside - now taller than the house itself. The bus came up to the window. The terror built, and as the window fell in, so did the front of the house. There was no escape. I knew the game was up. As the bus screeched into my bedroom.* I woke up under the blankets. I was frightened, sweating and shaking. It was still dark outside. I lay there, afraid to go back to sleep. But I must have because the next thing I remember, I woke up, and it was daylight.

One day, I was on the porch when I saw a man. He wore a dark suit and white shirt and had a dark blue tie. He wore dark, thick-rimmed, square-shaped glasses. He seemed as tall as my dad. His eyes were dark brown, and he had black hair, neatly combed, and was quite slim.

"Hello," I said.

"My name is Tom," he smiled. "I am glad you can see me."

I thought about that. "Why would I not see you?" I asked him. "Are you a magic man? Invisible to everyone but me?"

Tom laughed. "I am here to look after you." He told me. Seeing the puzzled look on my face, he went on to explain. "Stephen, I am not here to take you away from your Mummy and Daddy. I have come to see you as you are a very special little boy." Tom stood there looking round the porch. "I want to tell you that there are a lot of things you will see but maybe not understand." I had no idea what he meant.

"What do you mean? My sister told me I am her very special brother."

Tom sighed. "Do you remember seeing people in the fire?" He could see by my reaction I did remember. I thought about it. The lady with the shopping bags, the man with the bowler hat on. "You saw those images in the fire. This is why you are very special. You have a gift, Stephen." Tom looked at his watch, which I had not noticed until he rolled up his sleeve. It seemed large, gold-edged, with big numbers on it. "Got to go now. I shall come by soon and talk to you again." Suddenly, he was gone!

My days were spent daydreaming and sometimes trying to help my Mum in the kitchen.

"My throat hurts me," I told Mum one morning; she asked me how much it hurt. "Does it hurt when you swallow?" she asked me gently with a worried look on her face. "I think we should go and see the doctor." Mum went to the telephone and rang the doctors. "We have to see the doctor in half an hour," Mum said. Getting my coat and shoes, she hurriedly got me dressed, and a short while later, we were on our way. To go to the doctor's surgery, we turned right out of our front gate and walked up the street. It seemed a long way, and my legs began to ache. Mum picked me up, and eventually, we came to the main High Street, where all the shops were. There was a newsagent, a grocer with the name 'Roberts' above the shop; Josephine's, the sweetshop, and then a church, where later I would go to Sunday School. At the end was a huge bushy garden where the surgery was. Mum took me inside, and we sat down in the small waiting room. There were a few other ladies with their children. The doctor opened her door and shouted, "Next, please." One lady immediately stood up and walked into the room with a little girl who did not seem very happy.

Eventually, after what seemed a very long time, it was our turn. "So how can I help you today?" the doctor asked my Mum. Her name was Doctor Randall. She was quite short, with her grey hair tied up in a bun. I had a bad feeling about her. Mum told her that I had a sore throat. Doctor Randal picked up what I thought was a pen. "Can you open your mouth really wide, Stephen? Put your tongue out like this." She put her tongue out and made a noise, "Arrrgh. Can you do that?" She asked. I opened my mouth as wide as possible and stuck my tongue out. With the little pen thing, she put a tiny light on. Looking into my mouth, she asked Mum if I had a temperature. Mum told her I was okay, apart from my sore throat. A minute or two later, the doctor sat behind her desk and began to write on a slip of paper. "Stephen has tonsilitis. Here is a prescription. If it continues after a week, come back and see me again."

On the way home, we went to the chemist. It was a very small chemist. There was a counter at the back of the shop and lots of medicines on the shelves. It had a strange smell, which reminded me of the times I had to go to London to see the doctors. I noticed some round little lollipops on the front of the counter, orange, red, and yellow ones.

"Would you like one?" The chemist asked me as he gave Mum my medicine. I looked at my Mum; she nodded, and I chose a red one that tasted of cherry.

"Say thank you," Mum said; I thanked the man. Mum did a little shopping in the Grocers on the way home. There were shelves full of goods; it was family-owned.

Most shops were independent in our village. The main street went right through the village, which was on a hill. All the shops, the doctor's surgery, and the church were on one side of the road. Opposite were fields, and a little further on was the estate where we lived. It was about half a mile from the village to our house.

Every two months, Mum would take me to the big hospital in London. "This is where you were born," she would tell me. I liked going on the little red trains, watching the scenery, and seeing taller buildings as we came nearer to the city. The train stopped at several stations. Then came the change to another red train. Going down the moving stairs was the worst part of the journey. Mum would always keep me close and tell me to hold her hand. "When I say step forward, Stephen, step onto the moving stairs." Holding her hand, I would step hesitantly on the moving stairs, and then woosh! Off we would go, down a steep incline to the bottom, where Mum would encourage me to jump off. After several times, I became much more confident. Jumping off the moving stairs was fun; jumping on them was a little scary.

Doctor Smelly was my favourite. She was so gentle and made me feel happy. Often, she would ask me to stand on a weighing machine in just my vest and pants. My height would be measured, "Stand still and straight against the door." Doctor Smelly instructed me. She was always smiling. I found her quite funny. There were lots of things she would ask me to do, like walking across the room, standing on each leg, and asking me if I could catch a ball. Then she might sit me on a couch, ask me to relax and pick up an object that looked like a small mallet. She tapped on my knee, and my leg shot out. Then, the other knee had the same result.

Making notes, the doctor then would address Mum. I had the feeling things were not as good as they ought to be. Another appointment would be made, and we would leave. I was often given a lollipop by Doctor Smelly, which was really kind of her.

I had another sore throat. Visiting the doctors in the village, Mum was told I had another case of tonsillitis. More medicine.

"Hello, Stephen," Tom stood on the porch. I was on my way out into the garden to play with my brother. The back door opened to the porch, which faced the next door's back door. Tom smiled. He still wore a dark suit and a white shirt and tie. Black-rimmed rectangular glasses, like everyone had in those days.

"Hello, Tom. How are you?" I asked politely.

"I am very well, thank you." He ran his hands through his hair. "I have come here to talk with you today."

Looking around the porch and peering into the kitchen, he went on. "Firstly, how have you been since I last saw you? Have you had any more bad dreams and seen anything else?"

I wondered how he knew about my nightmares, as I could not recall telling Tom about them.

I think he must have read my mind. "I do know about your dreams. I have been watching over you." Somehow, I trusted Tom; I knew he did not mean any harm to me. Even though Mum and Dad had warned us all not to talk to strangers, I did not see Tom as a stranger, more like a friend. "Stephen, you are a very special, gifted little boy. I would like to pass on a little advice - you will see visions," noting the look on my face, Tom went on to explain. "When you have nice dreams, you may see things which, when you wake up, you remember and happen in real-time. These are dreams that do come true. I call them vision dreams." Tom smiled. His face lit up when he smiled, and I felt so comfortable talking and listening to what he told me, even if it did not make sense. "Your nightmares are different. These vision dreams are like seeing the future while you sleep." He told me these were nothing to worry about. Later, I learned the visions were premonitions; they would protect me. I would know when the dreams began to come true in my life what to look out for.

With all this information, he left, but I saw him again a short while later.

My sister had started school and had lots of friends. Some of her friends, who lived on the estate, often came round to play. They played doctors and nurses, and I was picked by my sister to be their patient. They played other games with their dolls.

"Why has your brother got a wonky eye?" they asked. Susan told them I was born with it. Susan had a squint where her eye went inwards, but my left eye was so far out I felt it was in my cheek.

Then they would ask, "Who are you looking at?" which I thought was odd. I told them I was looking at all of them. I could not understand why they would ask me that.

Going to the eye hospital in London, I had several tests and found that my right eye was the one I used most. "His right eye is short-sighted." The doctors told my Mum. My left eye was damaged at birth, so I was not able to use that one. Everything moved when they covered my right eye. I also had a headache after a few minutes of looking out of my left eye. I could not read any letters on the screen. "The letters keep moving," I told them. Notes were written, and another appointment was made.

Susan would tell her friends I was a very special brother. "He cannot help having a squint," she told them. Her friends played happily after, and I did join in sometimes.

One day, Tom arrived on the porch. Bright and cheerful. It was springtime. He was smiling as usual, but I had the impression that he wanted to say something very important.

"Stephen, I hope you are okay?" he tidied up his tie and, taking off his glasses, cleaned them on a white handkerchief, then placing them back on, he nervously shuffled his feet.

"Yes, I am fine. Mum tells me I shall be going to school in September. I shall be going with my sister on a coach." Tom laughed. I had no idea why he laughed, but when he did, it made me laugh, too.

"I have some important news for you." Tom seemed serious, happy, and sad all at the same time. "Firstly, I know you will love going to school, but I have to tell you that this is the very last time you will see me, Stephen." I felt like crying.

"Is this the news you want to tell me?" I felt sick and wanted to hug Tom. I realized then what a great friend he was, even though nobody else could see him.

"No, that is not all the news." Tom sighed. "Stephen, your Mum is going to have a baby. You are going to have a baby sister. You are going to see pictures in your mind which will all come true. You have a very special gift, which you will find as you grow up." Tom looked around the porch. "I cannot come to see you again because if I keep coming to visit, you may end up in a lot of trouble. I will send other people to watch over you, although they will not appear to you as I have." He stepped in and cuddled me.

"Stephen, who are you talking to?" Mum was in the kitchen at the sink near the back door.

I looked at Tom, and he smiled. "My friend Tom". Mum looked into the porch.

"Where is he?" I pointed to where Tom was standing. "There is nobody there. Is this one of the imaginary people you speak to?" Mum asked.

I was indignant. "No, Mum, he is not a made-up friend; I can see him." I went on to describe Tom.

"Come inside," Mum insisted. "I need to talk to you." I turned to say goodbye to Tom. He waved and then disappeared.

I never saw Tom again.

Mum sat me down at the kitchen table. "I know you think you can see these people." Mum spoke softly; seeing the stubborn look on my face, she went on gently, "You know when we go up to London and see all the doctors?" she stroked my head. "If you tell them what you have now just told me, they may take you away from us. I mean both me and your dad, your brother and sister, and we may never see you again!" Mum went on to tell me about a "special hospital" where people who say they can see things and hear voices are locked up. I was told about a place called Borstal - a mental hospital where these people are sent. "Children can be sent there too. I do not want you to be sent there, Stephen. I need to ask you to not mention anything like this to any of the doctors."

Nothing was ever said about this again.

A few weeks later, we went to see Doctor Soddy.

"Why do I need to go to the hospital, and Susan and John do not have to?" I asked my Mum as we got on the bus. We always caught the red bus to go to the Underground Station. The number on the bus was 107; it was a double-decker. Mum told me it was a Routemaster. When we were finally on the train, Mum leaned over to hug me. "When you were born, at the hospital we go to, you were very small, and the Doctors were worried about you, Stephen." She looked in her handbag, pulled out a small mirror, and put some light pink lipstick on. "Susan and John were not as small as you were, and they do not need to see the Doctors."

"He seems quite a chatterbox," Doctor Soddy said. He had asked me to say a little about what I liked doing. Once I started, I just seemed to go on and on. Mum told the doctor I was always chatting or singing. "Happy little boy, but he does wear me out at times."

Doctor Soddy was not like any other doctor I saw. He mostly sat in his chair, asking Mum a lot of questions about me. Grown-up stuff, which I did not understand. Then, he would ask me to talk about certain subjects. For instance, what I liked best - my favorite food or whatever. Then he would ask me to do things like tap my fingers on the table in a certain way, clap my hands, touch my head and, nose and ears, copying what he did. After a few tries, he would write things in his notes and talk to Mum, and then we would make an appointment for another time.

Mum was really pleased that I did not talk about the things I was told not to.

In August, Mum gave birth to my baby sister, Carol.

That summer, we went on the first holiday that I can remember. We went on a steam train with my Auntie and Uncle. It was a very long journey from Elstree to Weston Super Mare. Uncle gave all of us a bag of opal fruits, which lasted the whole journey. The train stopped to fill up with water on the way; a big arm reached over the train and filled the tanks up, and then we were off again.

I remember staying in a white house near the seafront. Every day, we would walk to the pier, and John and I would go on the roundabout. It had swans to sit on. We often went on the beach, which Mum described as mud. "Look - see how the tide goes right out." Mum pointed to the horizon, but I could see nothing. John and Susan jumped and squealed with excitement; they could see the sea. One time, Mum took my hand, and we walked out to the edge of the mud; then she said. "We must stay here, as that mud is dangerous. You may sink in it, and when the tide comes in, you could drown." We watched as the sea began to come in. "Look how fast it comes in." Mum crouched down and pointed with her finger; I could just make it out.

We always sat under the pier, making sandcastles. It was an amazing holiday; the first time I saw the sea.

Chapter 3

School

My first day was both exciting and sad. I had mixed feelings. The best part was travelling on a coach to school with my elder sister, Susan.

I was both excited and nervous. Going to school was something Susan was always talking about since starting two years ago. "You will love going to school." Susan had a huge Cheshire cat grin on her face. "Stephen, I will look after you. You are my baby brother."

Mum helped me dress in my school uniform. White shirt, grey shorts, and socks, brown jumper with a yellow band round the collar. Mum helped me with a tie. It was maroon with white and maroon diagonal stripes. Black shiny shoes. I had a satchel, too. Mum put on a pair of black plimsolls, which were to be worn in school. "This is your dinner money." Mum put some coins into my hand. "Put this into this." And she gave me a little purse. I put the dinner money into the purse. Mum smiled. "Good boy, and here is 6d for the tuck box at school." She gave my sister some money too.

Susan, Mum, and I walked to the coach stop. It was not far. About 350 metres from our house. Just one road to cross, which was on our side of the road. "Hold my hand," Mum said as we stood on the curb to cross the road. It was a cul de sac, so not much traffic came down the road. "Look left and right, then left again, and if all clear, we can cross over." Mum stepped onto the road, holding my hand, and we crossed the road. Just a few meters further on were children standing, chatting, playing with skipping ropes, waiting for the coach to arrive. There were privet hedges lining the path.

A few minutes later, the coach arrived, and all the children cheered. A lady stepped down as the door opened. She had a clipboard. Calling out our names, we climbed up the steps, one at a time, and took a seat in the coach. Mum waited to see us on and waved goodbye as the coach left to take us to school. We went to the end of the road, turned right, and travelled the same way as the bus which Mum and I took when I went to the hospital.

The school was in a place called Wealdstone, which was near Harrow Weald.

We left the coach and walked through a gate into the playground. There were seats and a small roundabout to play on, and I saw a huge log, which wobbled when you sat on it. A bell rang, which was the signal for us to all stop what we were doing and walk nicely into school. Susan grabbed my hand. "When we go in, make sure you take your shoes off and wear the plimsoles." Inside the school was a cloakroom. I hung my coat up on a hook and changed into my plimsolls.

As we entered the school, the headmistress met us. "You must be Stephen." she smiled warmly at me. "Susan, you can come too. I need to show you your new class.

My first teacher was Miss Guy. She was a lovely older lady. She looked ancient. Miss Guy played the piano at the assembly. I sat at a desk next to a girl. The first thing I noticed was I could not see the blackboard clearly. The writing on it was just a blur.

We had exercise books, where we were asked to try and fill in letters, which was like joining the dots. I liked that.

Playtime arrived, and we all went to a tuck shop. To buy sweets. I sat down at a table.

"What is wrong with your eye?" It looks wonky." I looked up and saw a freckled-faced boy with light brown hair and a runny nose staring at me. Suddenly, there was a crowd of children in a semi-circle looking at me. "Thornton has a wonky eye." They chanted. Later in the playground, they would come around and ask me who I was looking at. I just stood there and replied, pointing to one boy, "You, I am looking at you." Then everyone would laugh.

"But your left eye is looking over there." Pointing to my left. I looked in the direction they pointed to. There was a weeping willow tree swaying in the breeze.

I began to feel like an outcast. The children were all able to do things I found hard, like running on a bench. I fell off. Running around the playground. I tripped over. Catching a tennis ball, I dropped it or missed catching it. There were so many things I found hard; the children began to call me all sorts of names. One particular one was Spazzy.

On the couch, travelling home, some of the children left their seats. Leaned over the seat in front of me and stared at me. "Oh, I see what you mean!" I had no idea what they meant. "He does have a wonky eye." Susan stood up in her seat. "This is my BROTHER. LEAVE HIM ALONE! Or I shall have to deal with you." Then she sat down.

The lady who was in charge of the coach. Turned round, in her seat at the front of the coach, and told everyone to sit down.

My first day at school. I felt happy to go and sad to think I would be picked on. When we arrived home, Mum gave us a bag of sweets. "How did your first day at school go?" Mum asked me. I thought of all the good things that had happened.

"I liked singing and playing in the playground. We played chasey, chasey." It is a game where a person is picked to run after everyone, and if they catch them, then they join up and, together, try to catch another. Eventually, there is a long line of chasers joined in a long line. I went on to explain. Then I told Mum how I was picked on. "They say I have a wonky eye." I sobbed. Mum hugged me. Sitting down on the sofa next to me, Mum tried to console me. "Stephen, it is not your fault you struggle. You are very special." That bit made me smile. "You have a squint in your left eye." She went on. "A squint is when one eye is not in the middle of your eye socket. But lots of children have a squint. Susan has a little squint. Her eye goes inwards. Your eye goes out, which is unusual, fairly rare." Mum wiped the tears from my face. "Try not to cry, Stephen. You are a very special boy."

That night, I had one of my nightmares again. This time, it was the one with me being chased by a double-decker bus. I found myself under the bedclothes when I woke up.

I often went to the hospital. Virtually every few months. This meant a day out of school.

December came. John's birthday was on the 7th. Dad decided to take us up to London. We were all excited and looking forward to going up to Selfridges, a huge store in London, to see Father Christmas. It was really busy. Mum and Dad told us to keep close to them. Dad took my hand, and Mum took Susan and John's hands. I did not feel well at all, despite the excitement. I had a headache, and my throat hurt. Seeing Father Christmas, I went all shy, and though John and Susan were excited, I felt quite poorly.

"My head still hurts me, and my throat hurts more. I feel cold." I told Mum. Mum took a look at me and fetched a thermometer. "Open your mouth." Mum put the thermometer into my mouth. "Now close your mouth gently, do not bite on the thermometer." I had done this before, so I knew how it worked. "You have a temperature. 102. Laying me down on the settee in the living room. "You also have a red rash." She phoned the doctor." He is coming out this afternoon to see you." I was shivering uncontrollably. Mum gave me some Disprin. "Drink this. This may help to bring your temperature down." Mum gave me a small tumbler with cloudy water in it.

Doctor Gooley arrived just after two. He took a look at me. "I am just going to lift up your tee shirt." He said softly. He has a little rash, and his glands are swollen in here,". He said, touching my neck glands. "He has a Scarlet fever." He exclaimed. Prescribing penicillin, he left to visit his next patient.

Christmas was always an exciting time for us. Susan would wake us up in the middle of the night. "Look, Stephen, Loo, John, Father Christmas has come!" Susan would hold up a stocking we had put on the bottom of our beds. Though it was dark, Susan would open the presents in her stocking, encouraging us to do the same. Mum and Dad told us later we awoke at around 2 a.m. We would go back to sleep and wake up at a more usual hour. Our presents were in pillowcases downstairs. Both Mum and Dad, looking tired, made us eat our breakfast before we all sat down in front of the fire, which Dad had set up, to open our presents. Most times, we had aunties and Uncles turn up for the day, so it was, as my dad used to say Bedlam. We just enjoyed playing with our toys. Had so many sweets I thought they would last for months. More like weeks, though.

Mum would bake her own mince pies, which were made with short-crust pastry. Also, the minced meat was homemade. There were all sorts of homemade cakes and biscuits. The Christmas tree seemed really tall, with 100's coloured lights which twinkled. There was cotton wool around the bottom of the tree to imitate snow, as well as some draped on the mantlepiece and windowsills.

Going back to school in January was something to look forward to. Susan and I met the coach and joined the children as we sang on the coach. The lady who checked us on was always cheerful. She had dark brown hair, which was often tied up in a bun. The journey to school took about 20 minutes to half an hour, depending on traffic. Often, we would arrive in the playground a few minutes before the bell rang to tell us to enter the school. This sometimes meant I was not able to play with my friends, who lived locally, at the school.

It's a new term, but the same old…

Playtime came, and once again, a small crowd gathered around to look at my wonky eye. Once again, they asked me, "Who are you looking at?" I answered the boy who asked me on this occasion. He was slightly taller than me and had black hair, a round face, and brown eyes. I noticed he was quite a bit larger than me.

"You, I am looking at you." He grinned, and everyone started to ask the same question. I really felt uncomfortable. I turned away, tears in my eyes. I did not want them to see how upset I was.

One day, Mum knelt down in front of me as I was getting ready to go to school. "Stephen, today at school, you will be asked to go to see a lady who is going to help you speak properly." I had no idea what this meant. On top of everything, not being able to do things that other children found easy, Mum was now saying I needed help in speaking. Mum saw the puzzled look on my face. "It is how you pronounce certain words and letters. You say budder when it is supposed to be butter!" Mum went on, emphasising the T in the word. "Try not to worry, Stephen; this is quite common. There are lots of children like you who are finding difficulty in pronouncing certain letters."

Later, at school, I was asked to go to see Miss Game, the headmistress. Finding myself outside her door, I knocked gently. "Come in." A friendly voice echoed through the door. I opened the door and entered the room. Miss Game sat behind her desk. As I entered, she came round to the front of her desk and greeted me. "Hello, Stephen." She gave me a nice, warm smile. "You look very tidy today. I understand you need to see a lady for speech lessons." Miss Game was quite tall, about the same height as my Mum. She had light brown coloured hair and wore glasses. She was very trim and smart. Wore a nice colourful dress and a jacket. "Come with me, and I will take you to meet her." I followed Miss Game to the school exit via the cloakroom so I could put my outdoor shoes on. The new lady was quite tall. She wore a dark-colored coat.

"You must be Stephen." She knelt down to my level. "I shall see you across the road to the building where your appointment is. The building was white and had a few rooms adjoining a small corridor. "Sit down on a chair. Another lady will see you in a minute." She instructed me.

A moment later, a lady appeared. She had reddish brown hair. She wore a brown cardigan. "Hello, Stephen. How are you today/" she asked me as I sat down in her office. I was told to repeat sentences after her. "Pitter patter, pitter patter, down comes the rain." Emphasising the T. "The rain in Spain falls mainly on the plain." There were other things I had to repeat. For several weeks, I had to go there every Tuesday morning, which meant me coming out of school during lessons for at least half an hour.

Of course, the bullying did not stop there. Now, because I was being taken out of school for speech therapy, the other children made fun of me, mostly at playtime. From being a boy with a wonky eye, I was now being called "dimmo." Because I could not see the blackboard nor the words on the big sheet at assembly, which we looked at to sing the songs, I found myself being singled out for unwarranted attention.

My nightmares continued.

I had terrible headaches, finding myself in the medical room, at school, lying on a couch, in the dark, with a book to read, if I wanted to. Mainly Rupert Bear. This began to happen a lot. I had no idea what happened. I just found myself in the medical room, from time to time, feeling sick, my head pounding, tummy hurting too.

At the end of the school day, all of us who lived in Elstree had to wait in the assembly hall for the coach to pick us up to take us home. We sat in different rows, according to the year we were in school. Susan sat three rows away from me. This would be her last year in infants before she moved up to the juniors.

If there were any out-of-school activities, because we lived so far away, we were not able to take part, which was upsetting for me.

One day, in the spring, I was standing just outside the porch. I was thinking about Tom. John was sitting on a trike and pedalling around in circles in the garden. I heard a buzzing sound and swatted a wasp. Next thing, I had a really bad pain in my neck just below my left ear. I went in screaming. Mum sat me down and took a look. "You have been stung by a wasp, poor thing." She rushed to a cupboard. "Here we are; I have a blue bag that will take the pain away." Mum smoothed something on the painful sting. It immediately felt better.

I began to get visions that late spring and early summer. I found myself either sitting or standing still. Reels of pictures flowed through my mind, often in black and white. Everything I saw came true. I thought of Tom one time while having a vision. This one was me falling over as I ran next door, picking me up to take me home. I had no idea why I should see this, as I could not see myself running away.

One day, I was not happy and told my Mum, "I am going to run away and go to the fair, where that kind man who runs the goldfish stand is. Mum went upstairs and gave me a carrier bag. "Here you are, Stephen. don't forget to put a change of underwear and clothes in this bag." I packed my bag. The reason why I felt unhappy was really down to me not being able to do the things all the other children on the estate could do. My brother and sister, too. I felt I did not belong, although my Mum and Dad told me they loved me as much as my brother and sister. I felt if I went to the fair, people would not know me and look after me as a normal boy. As a four-year-old, this went through my mind.

"Goodbye, Mum." I walked out the back door and started to run down the street. I had only one thing on my mind, and this was to go to the funfair. There were two roads to cross and the main one. The main road could get quite busy, although we lived in a village. I held on to my carrier bag and ran. Before I could get to the first road, I fell over, grazing my knees. Next thing I was up in the air, as our next-door neighbour lifted me up and took me back home.

Indoors, Mum was wiping her eyes. I could see she had been crying. "I honestly did not think you would run away, my little boy." Mum picked me up and hugged me. "Stephen, I love you. Sometimes, you get on my nerves." I thought about this.

"What are nerves?" Mum giggled. Putting me back down, she went on. "It just means, sometimes you keep talking, and I cannot concentrate on what I am doing," Mum said. "Now go and play with your brother. He wants to play with you."

John would be going to school in September. I was so excited to have my younger brother with me at school. Susan was moving up to the juniors, so it meant I would not be on my own. He was very bright, and when visitors came around, they seemed to talk about how John could do this and that. "Look how clever John is." They would say. I cannot remember anyone saying that about me.

The school began in September, and we all went to catch the coach.

The questions began again. "What is that lump on your neck? Your eye is still wonky." As if my eye would miraculously recover during the summer. I put my hand up to feel for a lump. It was just below my left ear. When they saw my younger brother, they all crowded around to look at him because we were very much alike. Mum usually dressed John and me in similar clothes. Strangers often thought we were twins.

I still took days out of school to visit the hospital in London. Mum would take me to see Doctor Smelly. I really enjoyed seeing her. She was a pediatric nurse. "How has Stephen been since I last saw him?" she would ask my Mum. Mum would say there was not much difference, although I had no idea what that meant. I went through the same routine I was asked to do on the previous visit. "Can you tap your fingers like this on the desk?" I watched her tap one finger, her thumb, then she put two fingers, followed by her thumb. I copied her. "That is very good, Stephen." Doctor Smelly smiled at me and glanced at Mum. "His response times are not quite right." The doctor then went on to explain to my Mum how my reactions were slowing down. I had no clue whatsoever what this meant. I had copied her movements, so why is she sounding concerned?

Another appointment was made.

School days were hard for me. I was not able to see the blackboard or the hymn sheets hanging in the assembly hall with words to songs that we sang to the piano, not being able to do simple things that other children found easy. I felt different. I felt lonely. "Thorntons a dimmo. Thorntons a spazzo." They would chant.

I cried with frustration. I began to think to myself that being born on the 13th of the month was the unluckiest date to be born. The chants followed me through into junior school.

When it came to choosing sides for football or any other games, I was the last one to be chosen. I would stand there while the captains of each team were chosen. I was never asked to be captain. They would call out the names, and then there was me, on my own. If it was football, they stuck me in goal. After a while, I became so good at goals that there were a few times I was chosen first. Even the school goalie, a little guy called Mark, acknowledged I was really good in goal.

I began to think I was being accepted.

However, having to go to speech therapy and up to London to see countless doctors seemed unfair. "What hospital did you go to?" I asked a boy one day, as he had not been at school for a couple of days.

"What are you on about?" the boy scoffed. "I was not well, so my Mum kept me at home. That is all". The boy ran up the corridor to see his friends.

"Just because you have to go to a hospital, it does not mean we all have to go, dimmo." Another boy walked up behind me. He was about my height. Thicker in build. "Look at you." He sneered. "You are such a skinny weed and not right in the head."

I did not know how to answer, so I ran off to get away. I know I was very skinny at that age. Mum was worried about me not being the weight I was expected to be at my age. My brother and sister were normal for their age, but I was not!

I was more aware of my inadequacies as I went through school and grew up.

I had so many sore throats, and the doctor in the village surgery repeatedly gave me penicillin. "He has another bought of tonsilitis." The doctor would say. Eventually, one day, my Mum packed a bag for me." You need to go to the hospital, Stephen. They are going to take your tonsils out.

We went to the hospital in London.

There were quite a few children in the hospital. Mum took me up to the ward, where a kind nurse took my hand and showed me to my bed. It was a strange bed as it had bars all around it. Mum placed my clothes into a bedside cupboard. The nurse told my Mum there was a room with a television where I could go and watch a program with all the other children. I sat down on the floor near the back. My favourite program was on the telly. Doctor Who. As it started, I turned around and saw my Mum standing near the door. I smiled and waved to her. Watching the program, I forgot about everything. I looked around at one point to find my Mum had gone. My vision became blurred as tears began to fill my eyes.

I spent a week in the hospital. One morning, a nurse took me into a little room, where she sat me on a counter. "I need to take some blood from you. Can you show me your left arm?" I showed her my arm and held it out for her. "I can see your artery and veins," she remarked, pointing to the purple lines in my arm. "Can you make a little fist for me?" I did, and then the nurse picked up a small needle with a glass vial attached. This was the first time I had a blood test.

I had my tonsils removed and my adenoids. When I woke up from the operation, a nurse told me I was going home that evening. I stayed awake, waiting for my Mum to come and fetch me. But she did not. The nurse got me mixed up with another patient. I remember Dad coming to visit. He had a bag of chocolate buttons. I pretended I was a lion behind bars, as my bed was like that, and crawled around making roaring noises. As I came to Dad, he would put a chocolate button in my mouth. Dad rarely visited, as he was busy working. So, this was a treat for me.

At the end of a week, Mum came. "You are coming home today." Packing my clothes into a bag, we said goodbye to the nurses. Mum gave them some chocolates, and we waved goodbye.

Little did I know at that time I would come back to stay in the children's ward many more times.

There were a lot of changes which would have a huge effect on my life.

What Tom had told me was about to come true. Particularly the visions which, once they began, seemed never to stop.

Chapter 4

The visions.

My horrid nightmares were beginning to haunt me more and more as I grew up. Often, four times a week, I woke up in a sweat and shaking from dreaming I was being chased by huge animals. As I got older, the animals seemed to grow in size. The elephants were like tall buildings, lions as big as houses, and their roar was deafening. The cheetahs, pumas, and all the other wild animals were huge houses too. And yet, as I ran, they seemed not to be able to catch me. The nightmares began to make me feel much more anxious and frightened. Often, I went to sleep thinking of nice thoughts, hoping these thoughts would change my dreams.

"Can John come out to play?" Three boys who lived on our estate looked up at my Mum as she opened the front door. Both John and I stood next to Mum at the entrance.

"Can we go it to play, Mummy?" we both asked. The boys looked at me with a scowl. I could almost read their thoughts. "Not you. Spazzo, we do not like you. We want just John to play with us." Mum smiled at the boys and asked them to wait a while. John rushed to get his shoes on. I stood there in the hall, tears filling my eyes. Mum noticed my reaction. Kneeled down and hugged me. "You can go out to play as well," kissing me on the forehead. "Go and get your play shoes on," I smiled and ran to the cupboard, where we kept all our shoes and put them on. I was so excited to go out to play. Mum made sure we had a coat, "Just in case it rains while you are out." Mum helped us put our coats on. "John, you make sure you look after Stephen. If you do cross any roads, hold Stephen's hand tightly." She went on. With a frown on his face, John led the way out of the front door. The boys were still there by our front gate.

When we had gone a few yards down the street, we all stopped! One of the boys spoke to John. "Why did you have to bring your brother with you?" The other boys were giving me a look like WE DO NOT WANT YOU WITH US. I felt like running home. I could not understand why I was not liked. John was just over a year younger than me. When I felt I was older, then I should be making sure he could cross the road, not the other way around.

"Stephen is allowed to play with me, and I am not going anywhere without him!" I was stunned; John stood up for me. The last thing I expected was John to tell them it was both of us. We played with a lot of other children on the large estate. Cowboys and Indians, and Romans, where we used the aluminium dustbin lids as shields. Once again, sides were chosen, and I was the last one. Sometimes, if there was an odd number, the side that was left with me had the odd one, too. "Stephen is short-sighted, a dimmo."

We all split up to hide and then make plans for how to attack the other side. I put some ideas in, but they, as always, took no notice of me. I was left to look after the camp as they went into the attack. Being labeled as a retard, they never saw me as a boy who could do anything at all. I waited in the camp. I thought about how I was unlucky to be born on the 13th of the month. An unlucky number. I began to dribble. Closing my eyes, I saw pictures in black and white. I saw some boys running across a road. A boy was lagging behind, and I saw a car approaching; the boy was in the middle of the road, and the car went by but clipped the boy, who fell over and hurt his knees and his left arm. The car does not stop. The pictures join together like a reel of film. Keeps repeating over and over. I count in my mind six repeats until it stops. I open my eyes and notice the boys have returned. "Look at the spazzo, he has dribbled. Oh, what a baby. Only babies' dribble." I wiped my chin with my handkerchief. "We are going up to the village now." The boys decided. I looked at John. He had a smile on his face. I knew he would be going. To get to the village, we had to cross a main road. I remembered my vision. Thinking about it, I realized we would be crossing the road I saw.

"I think we should all be very careful, crossing the road leading up to the village."

"Oh, my goodness, and why should we take care then, spazzo?" The boys asked.

I took a deep breath. I did not know how to tell them. I decided to say something, as even though they did not accept me as part of their team, I did not wish to see one of them nearly getting run over by a car. "I saw a vision. I could see you all crossing the road, but one of you is last to cross and gets knocked over by a car." I paused. Then, I quickly finished my vision. "Whoever it is, does not get hurt. Just grazed knees, and his left arm has a cut on it."

The first reaction was complete silence. Then, all at once, one boy, who was the leader of our gang, laughed. "You honestly think you can tell us this is going to happen today? He put his face right up against mine. I stepped back. "You are not just a spazzo, but a psycho too." He turned to the other boys. "Come on, let's go to the village.

As we walked up to the village, I began to feel nervous. What if I wondered, my vision did not happen? I was hoping, in one way, it was a false vision, yet I was hoping it would. I had to show these boys I was able to do things, whatever that was exactly they were unable to do. I had never had a vision before. John held my hand; I know he felt reluctant to hold my hand across the road. The other boys were able to cross without anyone helping them. Often, they would run across a road. I was shocked! Mum had always told us never to run across a road. "What if you fall over? "Mum would say. "If a car was coming, you may be run over and killed. So always cross carefully." To see the other boys run across the road was a surprise to me. We reached the point where my vision began. John grabbed my hand, and seeing the road was clear, we walked across the main road. The other boys followed, some running, so they arrived on the other side before we did. One of the last boys ran across and did not see a car coming toward him. As he ran across, the car clipped him, and he fell over. Grazing his knees and hurting his left arm. I watched it happen, just like I saw in the vision.

The car never stopped!

The boys stared at me. The one who had been hit by the car was rubbing his knees, then holding his left arm, all at once. I do not know what they were thinking. I just felt numb. I did not know whether to feel elated or sad. The lead boy stood there staring, it seemed, right through me. "You saw this before it happened". He stated the obvious. I had no idea what to say or do. I was feeling shocked myself. This had never happened to me before. Then I remembered what Tom had told me long ago. "You will see visions." He had told me. Nothing more was said about this episode. On the way home, the boys kept a reasonable distance from me. John had to walk with me, but I knew he preferred not to.

On another occasion, we were out playing, and I had another vision. This time, a boy was on a go-kart. We made our own go-karts in those days. Taking the wheels from the prams, our mothers did not need anymore, we would get a plank of wood, and with the help of our dads, we would attach the wheels to the wood. Getting some rope, we then tied this to the wheels for steering. Sit on the plank of wood, and after a good push, go whizzing down the pavement. It was great fun. The visions always played like a reel of film in black and white.

No idea why my visions were not in colour. The boy was on his go-kart, whizzing along at a good speed. Going round a bend, he oversteered and crashed into a wall. The go-kart fell to pieces, so it had to be rebuilt. I knew who it was. A fair-headed boy. When it came to his turn, I warned him not to go so fast, as he would fall off, hitting the wall at the corner of the pavement. The other boys laughed. Of went the fair-headed boy. Going as fast as he could. Coming to bend, his go-kart toppled over and hit a wall; he came off it. Badly bruised. Once again, I found myself the center of attention for all the wrong reasons. "You are a Psycho," they shouted. Then, with no reason at all, they blamed me for everything that happened. "If you had not told us this would happen, then it would not have." They reasoned.

I felt out of place, not wanted. I was fed up with being called names. Although I tried to fit in, I somehow felt I could not. Not being able to cross the road on my own was, in my view, a huge handicap. Seeing children much younger than me allowed to cross the road on their own was somewhat degrading.There were two gangs on the estate where we grew up. Often, we would fight each other. Both gangs built dens, and we respected them. However, one sunny morning, the leader of the other gang, a tall boy with black hair and a dirty face, came up to us with a few of his minions. "You can have our den if you like. We have no use for it now". He offered his hand for friendship. As our 'leader' accepted the offer, I had a bad feeling about this.The other leader departed, and all of us gathered around, discussing when we should move into the den. Privately, we acknowledged their den was a lot tidier than ours. I saw a vision where we were in the den, and the other gang attacked us. They accused us of stealing their den. In my vision, I saw a huge fight.

"This is a trap," I told my friends. "They will let us have their den, show us around it, and then at three fifteen this afternoon, surround the den and attack us while we are inside. They will say we stole the den".

The boys stared at me. "Oh yeah? Well, we do not believe you. They shook hands on it, and that means they are being honest!" Clive shouted. He was leading our gang. Most of the other boys in our gang laughed and agreed with Clive. I say most of them, as two others seemed to think hard.

"Stephen has said a few things that have come true," one boy whispered loudly. "Maybe it is a trap." Clive took command and told us to pack everything and go to the new den despite my warnings. I felt sick in my stomach, and as the day went on, I felt more uneasy and sick.

The time I saw the attack was fast approaching. "Tell you what, spazzo, you can sit in the den, and if they attack, we will double round and get them." I was not happy at all. I knew I was being set up as a dummy. However, I had no choice. I could have run home, but that meant crossing roads, and I had no confidence in crossing roads, as it had been drummed into me; my eyesight was not good enough to see how fast cars were coming toward me. I had to sit in the den and wait. My gang hid in the bushes, waiting for the gang. At 3.15pm on the nail, there was a commotion as the other gang swept into the area of the den and threw rocks and stones at it. I, being inside, had most of the rocks aimed at me. Had a rock hit my right knee. I yelled out in pain. Suddenly, my friends appeared, and as my vision played out, there ensued a massive battle between the gangs. They accused us, as I had predicted, of stealing their den.

The boys began to listen to me for the first time. There appeared to be a little more respect. Clive asked me one day shortly after. "How do you see these visions?" I stared into the sky for a moment.

"I just see them in my head. They are in black and white." I looked at Clive. I noticed although he may not have understood how I do believe he acknowledged I had a gift.

Chapter 5

The truth is out there.

Summer holidays were always the best times. Six weeks of no school, and if we were lucky, a holiday to the seaside. This summer, we were going on a long journey to Cornwall. “We are going to New quay.” Mum and Dad exclaimed. “You have to go to sleep when we put you to bed; no reading comics or talking, as we have to be up at four O’clock in the morning. It will be dark outside.” We went to bed on the eve of our holiday. All of us were so excited I was afraid I would not be able to sleep and not wake up in time. I went upstairs. Mum had told us to get our clean clothes out and put them on the bed so we did not have to look for them in the morning. “We are leaving at five, if not before.” I snuggled down and fell asleep.

The next moment, Dad came into our bedroom. "Wakey, wakey, time to get up and dressed." He spoke silently. "The girls are awake." I could hear Susan squealing with excitement. Carol, not quite two, was still asleep. While we had a quick breakfast, Dad loaded the car. "Be very quiet as you get into the car," Dad instructed us. "The neighbors are still sleeping, and it is very early."

A short while later, we set off on a 12-hour journey to Newquay.

Mum had a map. We sat in the back of the car; in those days, there were no seat belts. Following the instructions that came with the map, we eventually came onto a main road, the A30, which Dad told us was the road that would take us all the way down to Cornwall. We stayed at a B&B called 'Blue Gates'. The house had blue gates, so I thought that was a good name. There was a little doggy who sang if we sang a song to it. He would stand up on his back legs and join in. That holiday was the best one ever. We went to the beach virtually every day. We visited Truro, Mevagissy, Falmouth, and Foye, where we saw my dad's Auntie, who seemed so old. I loved the little quaint streets, full of gift shops. I felt I could live in Newquay. "You will come down to work here one day." I heard a voice in my ear. I looked around, and an Angel was standing right close to me. I was stunned.

"Who, who, who are you?" I asked. I often stuttered when I felt stressed.

“I am Josie.” She replied. I noticed she had dark brown hair, similar colour to mine. She was not too tall, about my dad’s height. She wore a blue dress, which shimmered. I knew she was an Angel as she had wings. Smiling, she gently took my hand and took me aside. “I have been watching you, Stephen. I know you are a troubled little boy. You are a very special little boy”. There we go again. Everyone seems to think I am special. My understanding of being ‘special’ was one is simple. Backward, retarded, brain damaged. I guess visiting a hospital every few weeks did not help in making me feel normal, like other children.

Seeing Josie felt like normal. After seeing the visions, I felt this may be the next thing to happen. "Stephen, I will show you many pictures. Visions and I will be giving you information which will be helpful to you." She held my hand. I noticed her deep brown eyes. I could melt into them. I smiled and tried not to laugh at the idea of melting into her eyes. " There are a lot of things going on which you do not understand. The nightmares will stop. When they do, there will …" Josie stopped speaking. "This is all too much for you." Noticing my concerned look. "When you are ready, I will show you more. I need to go now, Stephen. But do not worry. You have a unique gift. This is because you are unique. You are different from all the other children, including your brothers and sisters. I shall be watching over you." With this last word, Josie kissed me on my cheek and disappeared.

The summer holiday came to a sad end. Dad drove us down to the seafront so we could wave to the sea and say 'goodbye.' It seemed a long holiday, two weeks actually, going on forever. We often went away near the end of August, so when we went back to school, the term had already begun. I was now in the junior school. The teacher seemed quite strict. I sat in the front of the class, as I could not see the blackboard very well, being short-sighted. I often had to try and copy what was on the board from the girl who sat next to me. The teacher told me several times about this. However, I felt the teachers and other staff were looking out for me. I had no idea why, but if anything went wrong, a teacher would take me out, not to tell me off, but to just make sure I did not get hurt. When it was playtime, we often took sides for football. A local boy brought a football into school, and we would all line up. Two captains were chosen. I was never a captain. I was always the last one to be picked. "You can go in goal." My captain told me. Eventually, I began to get really good at saving and began to be recognized as a good asset. One day, I was the first to be chosen! I loved being in goal.

One afternoon, we were asked to sit in the corridor at one end of the school. "You are all going to see the school dentist!" our teacher announced. Forming a neat line of two, we were marched up to the end of the school and asked to sit down on the benches, which were placed there for us. I sat down. The teacher handed everyone a huge envelope. Inside was a card that had our dental records on it. I noticed some of the boys and girls were taking the cards out of the envelopes. Our teacher did not notice, or perhaps she just ignored us, not doing what she told us. Tell someone not to do something, and you can bet they will.

I took my card out of the envelope. This was a life-changing moment! I stared at the card. It had two red lines drawn in red crayon. In between the lines was scrawled 'Brain in July.'

The boy next to me snatched it out of my hand. "Oh, my Stephen *is* a Spastic, after all." He passed my card to the next child, and suddenly everyone, even those at the top near the door, was chanting, "Stephen/Thornton *is* a spastic, Thornton *is* a spastic." I sat there stunned. I had no idea what was happening.

"Give me that card," our teacher demanded. I could see the anger on her face. Taking the card from a girl at the far end, she passed it back to me. "I told you not to take the cards out of the envelopes." She exclaimed in a very stern voice. "When I tell you NOT to do something, I do not want to see you doing it." I really thought at one point she was angrier at me than the others. As I put the card back into the envelope, I noticed the words on the card. 'Brain injury at birth' Not 'brain in July'. Tears filled my eyes. I felt that my little world was crumbling all around me, falling apart.

The rest of the day ended in a blur. I had no idea what a brain injury meant. "Am I a spastic?" I asked myself. I was crying and not hiding my tears. I did not care anymore. Perhaps all the children who bullied me and called me names had a point. I was determined to find out. I would ask my Mum when I got home. I felt sad, angry, disillusioned, confused.

The boys and girls may have felt guilty or something. They were quite distant, not really speaking to me. I was happy about them not talking to me. I would not have been able to deal with it. Somehow, I was glad it was a Friday, as by Monday, it may be all forgotten.

Some hope!

Mum noticed my wet face as I walked in from school. I ran up to my bedroom; John was behind me. Changed into my play clothes and lay on the bed. Tears fell down my face.

Mum came into the bedroom and sat down on the bed. "What is wrong, Stephen. Why are you crying? Susan and John said you are really upset."

I lifted my head, sobbing and looked at her. "What is a brain injury? I stammered. I shook as the tears rolled down my cheeks. I saw Brain injury at birth on a card when we saw the school dentist. Everyone says I am a spastic." I cried even more; my body shook as I sobbed uncontrollably.

Mum took my head and held me to her bosom. "When your dad comes home, we shall explain everything which you need to know." I felt Mum was upset. I did not know why. "Can you come downstairs? I shall get you some tea. Your favourite program is coming on soon. Crackerjack!"

Wiping the tears from my face with a flannel, we went downstairs. Susan and John were playing, and the television was on, too. We all watched Crackerjack and, after tea, sat up for a while.

Mum, Dad and I sat down at the table in the kitchen. Susan and John were told to stay in the playroom. I sat there quietly, feeling nervous and excited. I do not know why I felt that way. Perhaps it was because everything would become clear as to why I had to go and see doctors in London when both my sister and brother did not. Being born on the 13th seemed to bring a lot of bad luck. Dad took a sip of tea. Mum, her hands on her lap, twiddling her fingers nervously. I thought, if they were nervous, then perhaps I should be too.

"When you were born," Dad began, "or should I say hatched!" he laughed. Mum gave him a dirty look. "You were very tiny. Only 3lbs 15oz, and because you were so small, you were placed in an incubator. You were in an incubator for three weeks." I had no idea what an incubator was, and they went on to explain. Mum told me I was born with a brain injury and told me I was not expected to live.

"The Matron, sisters, and everyone did not expect you to be alive the next morning," Mum added. They dressed you in dolly clothes, as you were so tiny. They gave you the last rites every night, and you were fed intravenously by a tube." I sat there stunned, not knowing whether to laugh or cry. I was so ill, they went on, they were told not to expect me to be a normal child. If I lived, which was far from expected; apparently, the odds of me surviving were very low. I would be a spastic. That word again.

"What is a spastic?" I interrupted them. Being called that at school angered me. "They call me a spastic at school. Am I a spastic?"

They both stared at each other. "No, you are not a spastic!" They both told me. "We were told if you were spastic, you would not expect to be able to walk, run, speak or do anything for yourself. Live life in a wheelchair and may not be able to feed yourself." I had no idea how to react. This was a shock to me. Mum explained I was indeed a very lucky boy. "You may have cerebral palsy."

I did not feel lucky. Having all this going on, being bullied and, to top it all, never being asked to go out to play and not being allowed to cross the road on my own.

Dad told me on my birthday he did the football pools. He always did the pools on a Wednesday, but on my birthday, he decided to do them then. "I won some money, and because you had been so ill, I took you away on a week's holiday. You brought me luck."

All this news seemed like a fairy story. They had not finished with their story yet. After a few weeks at home, I was screaming nonstop in pain. Dad used to walk me around the house, trying to calm me down, but I kept on and on. Mum took me to local doctors, who told them I had a severe case of croupe. Mum had a 'feeling' there was something more sinister going on. She noticed that I was vomiting up brown stuff after every feed. Taking me to University Hospital, where I was born, they discovered I had a hernia. A small operation was needed.

My luck was with me; one day, when I was six months old, after a feed, Mum told me. "I took you out of your highchair, took you into the living room and thirty seconds later, I heard a bang. Going back into the kitchen, I saw an air gun pellet in the high chair. If I had not picked you up, you would have been dead. That is another reason why you are a lucky little boy."

Dad finally explained he had a brain injury. I found that hard to believe, as Dad was in management and was very highly thought of in his job. He told me not to expect to get anything easy. "You had a fight for survival as a baby. When everyone, including us, did not expect you to live, you fought and fought to prove us all wrong. And you have, Stephen." Almost reading my thoughts, "John can see better than you, and that is why he is given the task to look after you when you cross the road. The doctors say," Dad paused for breath. More slowly. "You have short sight, as you know. When it comes to crossing the road, we have been advised by the doctors you cannot see the distance cars are approaching you." I remember Mum telling me this a long time ago. When we were crossing the road to catch the bus, Mum used to ask me how long a car in the short distance would pass us. I was useless at seeing the car. They added due to the squint in my left eye, I was unable to be given glasses to wear like other children. I was not allowed to cross a road until I was at least 12 years old.

Well, that was all they had to say. I sat there stunned. There seemed to be more questions than answers. "Wha wha wha is cebral pa.....?" I stuttered.

"You know that lady whose head keeps nodding up and down?" Mum asked me. I remembered seeing a lady who seemed to be nodding all the time. "She has what is called Cerebral palsy. It is where you cannot control certain actions." Mum went on to explain that I was lucky not to be affected by this condition.

I never forgot that day. It was like a curtain being lifted, a light being switched on. Knowing all this was also a great weight being taken off my shoulders.

However, I still felt the same little boy. Different, not fitting in.

The bullying never stopped.

The nightmares continued to scare me.

Things on a daily basis never changed.

I changed. I began to understand.

One day, I told myself, all these bullies will find out how clever I can be.

Chapter 6

Osteomyelitis

Christmas came, and the family, as usual, had an exciting time. Dad would decorate the house with cotton wool around the base of the tree, on the mantelpiece, crepe decorations across the ceiling with tinsel hanging down, and paper decorations also hanging from the ceiling. Christmas was always a magical time for me.

We woke up on Boxing Day. Outside was a thick blanket of snow! Our hedge in the front garden was white. The snow was so deep we virtually sank in it. Often, we found the bus or coach which took us to school was caught in a drift, so that year, we often stayed at home. The snow stayed around until the middle of April.

The following summer, we went to Devon. This was another adventure. Leaving home in the early morning, we took a similar route to last year. "Exmouth is in Devon; it is not so far as Newquay. No Atlantic rollers." Dad added.

The week we spent in Exmouth was exciting. We stayed in a B&B close to the seafront. The beach was huge and very long. There were rock pools and sand dunes. There was a funny-shaped ice cream parlour on the promenade, which

Mum said was called the Octagon. It was eight-sided with four serving hatches. We often went into a tearoom. This was above a bakery in the town. We have to be on our best behaviour. The town had a green area in the middle, where the cars drove around. There were also some shops where we bought our food for the day. A little supermarket and a bookshop.

All too soon, the week passed by. As we left the beach on the last day, Mum remarked how tidy and clean the town was. "No litter anywhere. I would love to retire here, Bernard. This is a really lovely area".

Josie appeared. "Tell your Mum she will retire down here with your Dad. Not everyone will come down. There is a brother, and your baby sister will come down with them. Susan will not, neither will John, but YOU will a few years later."

As we walked up the steps from the beach, I repeated what Josie had just told me. My parents smiled. "We shall see." They both laughed. "It would be nice to come here for a walk in the evenings," Dad remarked. "Yes, I agree, a nice place to retire."

The girl next door had a rabbit. A rabbit. They passed it over to my sister Susan to hold for a minute. Passing it to me, I held it in my arms. "We need to go now. Teatime." The girls said. They reached out for the rabbit, which I held in my arms. As I handed the rabbit to them, it scratched my right hand with its back legs. It bled a little, and I thought no more of it.

A few weeks later, I had a cut on my left finger, which became painful. "My finger hurts me." I cried as I touched the bruise. It was turning yellow. Mum took my hand and gently lifted the bruise.

"Oh my, it has gone septic." Getting some iodine, she gently diluted it in water on a soft cloth and wiped the area. "I do not know how this bruise has gone like this."

I was still having my recurring nightmares. I was chased by ferocious monsters, roaring as I ran and ran to get away. "Stephen, do not cry so." Josie appeared. She caressed my face. "I know these nightmares are terrifying. You may not know why you get them, and your brothers and sisters do not. You will find out one day the meaning of these nightmares."

"Do you know why I have these nightmares?"

Josie rubbed her hand through her hair. "I do know, Stephen. But if I tell you now, you will NEVER understand. You are not ready for this at the moment. When you are old enough, I will show you, and then it will all make sense." She took my hand. Her hand felt warm and soft. "You have a long, hard journey ahead." She looked deep into my eyes. "I know you feel unlucky, being born on the 13th; that is not an unlucky number. I know you're being made fun of, so try not to worry". I am always by your side." Josie sighed. "You have a very special gift, Stephen. You can see the future. You already have seen visions, have you not?

I thought about the go-kart, the den and how I saw the other gang attacking us.

"You will be shown many more visions, Stephen. She kissed me, and suddenly, Josie was gone.

Later that year, Mum asked me if I had cleaned my teeth. "Your breath stinks." She moaned.

I always cleaned my teeth and could not understand why I had stinky breath. Even my brothers and sisters noticed. One Saturday evening, a tooth fell out. Holding it in my hand, I noticed it looked rotten. Mum immediately took it and, examining the tooth, told me to throw it in the bin. "This tooth is rotten. It stinks!" I sniffed, and indeed it stank. Throwing it in the bin, I asked, "Is this why I had stinky breath?"

"Come over and sit on my lap." Open your mouth." I did as she asked. "Yes, I do believe the tooth was the cause of your stinky breath."

In January, I went downstairs to the kitchen. Mum was washing up. "My foot hurts."

Mum asked me to show her my foot. I took my slippers off and put my right foot forward. Pointing to a tiny lump on the bone on the big toe, "This lump hurts a little bit."

Mum touched the lump. "Does it hurt when I touch it?" She had a concerned look on her face.

"No, it just hurts now and again," I replied. "It is not like the lump on my neck. That does not hurt."

"Okay. We shall see how it is over the next few days," Mum stood up and wiped her hands on a cloth. "Now finish getting ready for school, as the coach will be coming soon."

At playtime, the boys all decided to play football again, this time with a tennis ball, as the boy who often brought the football in was not at school. We chased the tiny ball around. I was stuck in goal as usual.

I picked up the tennis ball and kicked it. Ouch! My big toe hurt. This time, the pain was like a sharp needle in the bone.

Mum took me to the doctor the very next morning. She had a concerned look on her face. Another day off school! Doctor Randall was the local GP in the surgery. "I do not like her," Mum whispered as we sat in the waiting room. I was rubbing my toe as I felt the dull, achy pain.

In the surgery, Doctor Randall immediately asked me to raise my chin. Reaching for a light, she looked up my nose. When did Stephen have his nosebleed?" she inquired. Mum, I could see, was quite annoyed.

"He has not had a nosebleed. He has a lump on his toe, which is painful." Mum replied indignantly. Doctor Randall hurriedly placed her light on her desk and studied my right toe. Mum had already taken my shoes off.

"Mmm, how painful is it?" The doctor touched the lump. It was bright pink. I flinched and took my foot away. She rose and sat at her desk. Writing notes and a prescription. "I have prescribed a course of antibiotics for him. Should this not clear up in a week, then bring him back."

We left the surgery. I was limping a little. A week passed, and my toe became even more painful. The bones in my foot were not so visible as the whole foot began to swell. I could not get my slipper on. The next few days went by, and the pain became unbearable. Imagine putting a red-hot poker on your toe and leaving it there.

I screamed!

I slipped into bouts of delirium, and the only respite from the agony was when I was asleep or in an unconscious state due to the pain. Days turned into weeks. I hopped around on my left foot. I could not place my right foot on the floor. If I did, the pain was unbearable. If I dropped a tissue paper on my foot, I screamed in agony.

During the worst bouts of delirium, Josie visited me. I was so happy to see her. She made me feel comfortable. Caressing my face, she helped cool me down. "You are very ill," she whispered to me. "I have been around you every day. Your Mummy is very worried about you." I lay there in so much pain I could not focus at all.

Doctors came and went. They had no idea what was wrong with me. I have never seen a patient with the condition I was suffering with.

Weeks passed, Easter came and went. I had no idea what month or day it was.

One day, Doctor Gooley made one of his many visits. I was in bed with a chair over my foot. I slept with a chair as the sheet touching my toe was too much for me. He touched my right toe very softly. I screamed in pain and nearly passed out. "Mrs Thornton, I feel Stephen is a brave little boy. I have never seen anyone in so much pain. I have asked my colleagues at the hospital if they know or have any idea what is wrong. I am sorry, but they could not help me." Mum was standing on the other side of my bed. I lay there sweating in pain and wished at that moment I could go to sleep and never wake up again.

Suddenly, another Angel appeared in the bedroom. I had never seen this Angel before. He was quite tall, around 6ft in height. He had wavy brown hair and a beaming smile on his face. Hazel eyes. He was dressed in green. He stood next to Mum and spoke in her ear. Then, as suddenly as he appeared, he went.

"Could it be osteomyelitis?" Mum suddenly asked. The doctor stared at my Mum.

"Who told you this?" doctor Gooley reached into his bag. He brought a huge compendium. Mum replied that this just came into her head, "I do not know how this came, but a voice just told me Osteomyelitis".

Doctor studied his book, turning pages over. "I believe you are right, Mrs Thornton. How did I miss this? I do not know. It all makes sense. You mentioned a bad tooth, and the symptoms do mention a rotten tooth." He rose from his chair and, with Mum's consent, hurried downstairs to call for an ambulance. A short while later, the ambulance arrived, the bell sounding as it drove up our street. I was stretchered downstairs into the ambulance. Some neighbours were looking at what was going on. Putting on the blue lights, the ambulance took me to hospital. Mum was with me, and a paramedic, too. We arrived at Stanmore Orthopaedic Hospital, the one we travelled past on our way to London and to school. After a thorough examination, it was agreed I had a very rare disease. This was so rare that most of the consultants had not seen it. They had read about it and knew it was a disease that, if not caught early, would kill the patient. Of course, I became an exhibit. I did not see the funny side of this. I was in too much pain to even think about how rare the disease was. I just wished I could be free of the pain.

I was finally taken into hospital at the beginning of May.

I spent a whole month in the hospital. The day I went in was horrible. I screamed in pain. I began to lose consciousness. I wanted it to magically go away. To wake up with no pain.

The doctors crowded around my bed in the ward. It really was an exhibit! The consultant in charge had student doctors with him. 'Do not touch my toe', I implored. They did not. Mind you, they got really close to seeing it. "Tomorrow, you shall have a small operation and wake up with no more pain." The consultant smiled and turned to his students. "This is a very rare case of osteomyelitis; in your lifetime as a doctor, you may never see this again!" The consultant then asked them to take a good look at my foot. "See how swollen it is. This boy has been very lucky because if we left it much longer, there may not have been much more we can do for him". He gave me a warm smile and went to another child to examine.

I woke up after the operation and had a plaster cast on my leg. From my foot, not covering my toes, up to just below the knee. The good thing was I was in no pain. I pinched myself. Not having any pain after months of agony. This was a blessing.

A nurse came to see me. "I see you have woken up," she gave me a nice warm smile. She had light brown wavy hair. Hazel eyes and was very slim. She had an upside-down watch on her right, and she looked at it as she took my wrist. "Just checking your pulse." Then she looked at my toes. "I bet you are happy not to be in so much pain". Giving me another warm smile. "Now, Stephen, you have to be a brave boy. "I have to give you an injection, which may be a little painful. However, not as painful as your toe was." Reaching into a shallow utensil, she brought out a needle. "Where would you like me to inject you? She asked me gently. "In the top of your knee?" she touched me where she intended to put the needle in. "or in the side of your leg up here?" She touched me on the top of my leg near the thigh. I decided to have the injection in the side of my leg.

To say it hurts is an understatement. It was really painful.

Over the next month, I had those injections every six hours. Day and night. My legs on both sides turned purple. My plaster cast was changed, and they put what they called a rocker on it. This enabled me to walk on it. In all that time, I was stuck in bed.

I finally came out of the hospital at the beginning of June. I then spent a further two weeks with my grandparents, who lived in Bromham, Bedfordshire, a good hour's drive from our house.

I spent a lovely time away, and my grandparents took me out virtually every day.

One day, I received a postcard from Mum and Dad. As I read it, I burst into tears. They had gone to see a film, which I wanted to see. I never saw that film until many years later. I know Josie was with me; I saw her appear as I walked into the garden. Grandad had a huge garden. He grew vegetables in a small orchard, blackberry bushes, and other soft fruits. The top of the garden had an aviary, where he kept Red Factor canaries.

"I am glad you are happy." Josie took my hand as she usually did. "You are such a brave little boy," she walked around the garden with me. It was such a warm, sunny day. "One day, you will find true happiness. The bullies will go away, and you will be famous. You will write the book you dream about. I shall help you." She kissed me on my forehead and disappeared.

I went back to school for the first time since the middle of January. I still had my plaster cast on. It was now the beginning of July. Only a few weeks until we broke up for the summer holidays.

I found it very hard to settle. I was not allowed out in the playground due to my foot being in plaster, so someone had to sit with me up near the headmaster's office. I felt guilty. I was depressed and was unable to stay focused in class.

When I finally had the plaster cast removed. I felt like my leg was as light as a feather. I noticed how white my skin was. I suppose one notices these things when one has had a plaster cast covering. I found it hard to walk properly. I had a pronounced limp. I was glad the school year ended. I wanted to stay home.

Little did I realise my days in the hospital were going to increase.

Josie appeared again. Her hair flowed down her back. She glided toward me. "Stephen, you are going into hospital early next year and also, I have to say, you will go into hospital for an operation on your eyes to fix the squint. "Once again, she took my hand. "I am always with you. If you ever want me to come, just call my name. I shall answer your call."

I was taken aback! "Why are you telling me this? I stared at Josie. "You have me worried now."

Josie caressed my face. "Stephen, I do not wish to alarm you. You are being told this because you are gifted and, in the future, you will be shown and told many things which will come true. Not just for you, but for people who you will meet in years to come." Josie sighed, looked momentarily at the sky, and then back to me, giving me a huge smile. "There are other Angels who want to help you. They will come into your life when you are ready. I shall be with you always."

The next year, the lump on my neck began to hurt. I went into the hospital for an operation, as it was diagnosed as an abscess. More time off school and a two-week stay with my grandparents.

Chapter 7

Dreams and visions.

The nightmares, which I had since I was a very young boy, continued. Although, by now, one may think that by being used to them, the anxiety would diminish. I can honestly say it did not. Fear took over, and though the recurring nightmares came virtually every night, they had the same effect as the first time I had them.

One evening, Dad took John and me out to see a film. We went by two buses. On the way back, we went upstairs on the double-decker. Dad and John sat opposite me together. I sat on a seat on my own. It was dark. I began to dribble and saw a black-and-white vision.

Dad was telling us to follow him down the steps to the platform below. He explained to us he would ring the bell. The bus slowed down; Dad told us to skip off the bus. The bus slowed right down; Dad skipped off the bus, and John followed. The bus began to speed up again. I jumped off and fell over on the road. I saw a white car with rectangular headlights coming towards me. (Rectangular headlights were very uncommon.) As the car approached, I was frightened. I thought I was going to be run over. Instead, the car went by. I felt the air as it sped by. If I reached out, I knew I could touch it. I got up and saw both John and Dad laughing.

Like all my other visions, this played over and over like a newsreel.

"Are you okay?" Dad asked me. "Wipe your chin, you are dribbling." I wiped my chin. I explained what I saw in my vision. John giggled.

Dad rose from his seat. "Come on, boys, follow me down the stairs. Be careful as you may slip." I think that was aimed at me. We followed Dad down the steps onto the platform. Dad rang the bell. "When the bus slows down, skip off the bus like this." He did a little skip. "This way, you should not fall over when you land on the pavement. This is just in case the bus does not stop."

The bus slowed, Dad skipped off, and John followed as the bus began to speed up again. The vision came into my mind. I jumped off the bus, fell over in the road, and looked up to see a white car with rectangular headlights speeding towards me……..

We moved to St. Albans. It was a Roman town where Mum and Dad often took us shopping when we lived in Elstree. Dad had a new job in the bank, so we could afford to move. On the day we moved, it snowed. The house was next door to a junior school. The end house in a cul de sac. There were only eight houses, and we were number 8.

Susan went to a school on the other side of town. Because I was not allowed to cross the road, I went to a school for boys just around the corner.

I hated it!

The bullying started from the moment I walked into the school. I still had a squint. "What is wrong with your eye?" They would all gather around me. I was labelled a retard as I was unable to do things the other boys could.

I hoped all the bullying that I went through at my last school would stay there. Unfortunately, it did not.

In January, just as Josie had told me a few years ago, I went into hospital again. This time, I had to have my squint repaired. Three weeks off school.

However, following the surgery, I was prescribed glasses. At last, after all the years of not seeing the blackboard, I was able to see words and numbers written on it.

One morning, a boy who came round to walk with me to school rang to say he would be a little late. "Did you have an egg for breakfast?" I asked him as we spoke on the telephone. He told me he had.

"Why are you asking me?" he inquired.

"You have some egg on your clean shirt," I replied. This was met by silence, and then he came back with a question.

"Are you psychic? I just noticed some egg down my shirt." When we walked to school, Josie came with us. The boy, who was a good friend, was talking nonstop. "How did you know I had an egg for breakfast?" I am not sure if he was asking me or talking to himself. When we reached school, I asked him not to mention this. But he did! I became the focus of attention I did not want. Everyone, including the bullies, picked on me. What am I going to have for dinner? They would ask.

Just after my 14th birthday, my nightmares ceased. Just as Tom had told me all those years ago.

The dreams I had then were strange but not frightening.

I was in a temple. It was quite dark. There were lighted candles on the walls. I looked around and saw a figure standing in the shadows. I could not see who it was, but I did not feel threatened. The figure slowly came towards me. It was tall, about 6ft. I noticed there were scrolls of parchment in its hands. As it came closer, I noticed it was an Angel. He looked like a monk. He had a dark brown cloak wrapped around him. His head was also covered. Giving me the parchment scrolls, he signalled me to open one. I did. There was writing in a strange language, Hieroglyphics. "These scrolls are for you." The Angel whispered. I studied the writing, not understanding what the words meant.

This dream came often to me. Sometimes, I saw the writing on the walls of the temple. I could sense the Angel near me, even if I did not see him. For the next 10 years, this dream would recur.

I left school and was so happy to walk out for the very last time. Shortly after leaving school, I had very strange dreams.

I saw a friend driving a car which crashed, and he was crippled by having a permanent limp. Another boy from school was riding a bike. He was involved in an accident with a car, which hit his bike. The boy died. In another dream, I saw another boy run across the road and was killed by a lorry which was speeding.

Later, these dreams come true. I was shocked! I asked myself why I was dreaming of these events. I did not understand why I had these dreams.

Josie came to me one day as I sat on my bed. "You are being shown future happenings in your dreams. These are called premonitions."

"Why?" I asked her. "Could I have prevented this? My friends have been killed in nasty road accidents, and they are not even old enough to die." I was very upset.

Josie sat down next to me. "No, you could not have." Seeing the concerned look on my face, she explained. "Stephen, just suppose you had warned them about the dreams you saw. Would they have believed you?" I frowned. "They possibly had laughed at you. Made fun. But this is something you could not change." Josie took my hand. Hers were quite warm. "You will have other premonitions. Some in dreams, some in visions. Some you will be able to change because they will involve you. Others you cannot change, but you should not worry. You are such a gifted young boy." Josie rose from the bed and disappeared as she usually did.

One day, I was walking home from the shops. I was nearing my home when suddenly Josie appeared next to me. I went shopping as I was so surprised to see her. I am 19 years old now. Had a nice job buying and selling books for a local wholesaler. "I have some news for you, but please do not be alarmed." Josie smiled at me. "Two weeks before your thirty-sixth birthday, you are going to die." Josie took my hand, seeing how concerned I was. "Please try not to worry about this."

I picked up my shopping and began to walk home. I was very worried. "Why are you forecasting my death?" I replied.

I was nearing my house at the end of the road. Josie stopped. "It does not mean you are going to die, but in a way which I cannot explain, you will."

I watched Josie as she disappeared.

Mum was pleased I managed to get the groceries. I told her what I was given by Josie. Mum grimaced. "Stephen, I wish you would not go around saying horrible things like that. You are not going to die. Well, not at that young age." Mum began to walk around the kitchen. I felt she was agitated. "After all you have been through as a child, you joke about dying at 35 years."

I did not know what to say. I went up to my bedroom and played some records.

Often, my friends would ring me and ask if I was happy to join them. I had some good friends, although they still made fun of me. Outside our clan, if anyone else took a poke at me, then they would stick up for me.

Most Saturday nights, we would catch a bus from St Albans town centre and travel to Dunstable. There was a venue named The California Ballroom. Lots of pop groups performed there before going on a national tour around the country. The cost was just one pound. The first time we visited the venue, a top radio 1 DJ was the main performer. Noel Edmonds. Other top groups we saw were Chairman of the Board, Travares, The Sweet, The Drifters, and Suzie

Quatro, just to name a few. Even Slade turned up during their heyday.

One evening, we all travelled to the ballroom. We wore the latest gear. Platform shoes, coloured jackets and flared trousers.

Josie gave me a warning before I left home. "Be careful, as you are going to sprain your right ankle. Look, I shall show you." I saw a vision. We were leaving the ballroom a little later than we should have, and the bus, which left the stop at 12 midnight, was leaving. In the vision, the boys were running to catch the bus. I was hobbling in pain. We had to catch a taxi home.

I told my friends what I was shown. They laughed!

We had a really good time! Dancing to the band and drinking. One of my friends suddenly noticed the time. We took our coats from the cloakroom and rushed out down the hill toward the bus stop. The bus was waiting. We stumbled on our platform shoes. My right ankle gave way, and I fell over. A searing pain overwhelmed me, bringing tears. I could not walk, never mind about running to catch the bus. We finally found a taxi that took us all the way back to St Albans. Just as Josie had shown me in the vision.

After this happened, I had many more dreams and visions.

One Friday evening, my mates and I went to a nightclub in Leighton Buzzard. In those days, cars did not usually come with a radio fitted. My friend had a huge radio, which he placed firmly on the passenger side on the floor. Anyone sitting in the passenger seat could put their feet up on the radio. It actually worked once he had wired it in.

In the disco, the music was deafening. One had to shout to be heard. We were bopping to the music and having a wonderful evening. Chatting up girls and doing what lads usually did in those days. Near the end of the evening, I saw another vision. Two guys, one with blonde hair, the other shorter with dark hair, with jackets on, break into my friend's car and steal the radio. Despite the noise, I shouted to my friend, Alan, what I saw. He laughed. When we finally left, which was not long after, he went to unlock the car. The key did not work! "That is strange." Alan held the key in his hand. "I cannot unlock it."

I reminded him what I told him in the disco, not realising he had told the others. He tried opening the door. It opened. Peering inside, he exclaimed, "The radio has been nicked." As we all piled into the car before starting the engine, they all rounded on me.

"It is all your fault, Steve. If you had not told us this would happen, then it would not have."

I sat there stunned. "What do you mean it is all my fault?" I stared back at them. "Do you honestly believe I can make things happen by just predicting the future?" I was quite upset from one extreme, where they laughed at my predictions, to now blaming me for the robbery of the radio. It did not make sense.

It was soon all forgotten as we made our way back home. It was now 2am in the morning.

The next day, Saturday, the house phone rang.

“Stephen, it is for you.” Mum handed me the phone. “It sounds like your friend Lee.”

I took the phone. “Steve, how are you today?” It was my friend Lee. He had been with us last night. I told him I was fine. “Sorry about last night. I do not blame you. Are you coming over this morning?” We often met up on a Saturday morning. Mostly, we played songs on our guitars and watched Thunderbirds on the telly.

That morning was really nice. Lee’s Mum made me a cup of tea before we went upstairs to his room, where we played our guitars.

I still had my dream where I was in the temple. The Angel appeared as usual. In a brown cloak, dressed up like a monk. Showing me ancient parchment scrolls. I could not understand the writing. In the dream, I felt safe and comfortable. I somehow knew one day; the scrolls were going to be of importance to me.

Little did I realise how important they would be.

Chapter 8

Holidays with my friends

Some weekends, Rob, Alan and I would all jump in a car and travel down to Swanage. Rob had an elder sister who sang in a local pub down there. We would stay in a guest house and go fishing for flounder in Wareham, which was not too far away. One weekend, we travelled down as we were invited to an engagement party. Rob's sister was getting engaged. We all had a fabulous time, drinking, dancing, and just having a lot of fun. Rob's parents went down, too.

The party finished around midnight.

Josie came to me. "Hello Steve, you are going to be asked to drive a car, as the driver is not well. They will pay you for driving their car home". Josie looked a little worried. "The car will break down, and you may not get home until 4am in the morning".

Later, the party broke up, and everyone was leaving. One of Rob's relatives approached me. "Can you help us out?" he asked me. The guy was one of Rob's uncles. Balding head and round face, red with too much drink. I stood back, just in case he was going to fall over, and I did not wish to get in his way. His wife and a few other characters approached. Rob's mum pulled me to one side.

"Stephen, would you be able to help us? If you can drive their car back to St Albans for them, I will be very grateful". Rob's mum always treated me like another son. "He has drunk too much, and the other one who was supposed to drive also is off his head. I am sorry, Stephen."

I agreed reluctantly. Thinking about what Josie had told me.

We all left Swanage in our cars. We came to the big hill, and the car slowed down. Struggling to get up the hill. I changed gear and, after a time, realised the clutch had gone. Eventually, we had to stop. The owner of the car was in the passenger seat, not the best for wear, and was thankfully a member of the RAC. Finding a phone box, he rang them. An hour later, the RAC turned up. Finding it was the clutch, the guy ordered a recovery van to take us home. Another long wait. I was cold and tired. The others in the car were either fast asleep or moaning about the car. That did not help me. A good while later, the recovery van turned up, and we were soon on our way. We arrived in St Albans at 5.30 am.

Rob's family lived on the other side of town. One of his relatives gave me a lift home.

I knew Josie was looking after me, but I also knew somehow things which she warned me about I could not control.

One summer, my friends and I all decided to go to a holiday camp in Cornwall. It was on the North Coast, not too far from Lands End. A place called Skewjack. Renowned for having one of the safest surfing beaches in Cornwall. We stayed in tents supplied by the campsite. We all travelled down in different cars. Lee and I in his, Rob, Alan and a few others in Alan's car and the rest in another car. There were 12 in all. Lee and I lost our way. We travelled down the A38, missing the A30 turnoff. But we arrived there in the end. In fact, we were the first ones to arrive, shortly followed by Alan and Rob, with some of the rest.

We had all agreed to stay for two weeks. The tent we stayed in was huge. We laid out our sleeping bags, deciding where we were going to sleep. Lee was next to me, as we were best friends. We had brought our guitars on holiday. Everyone loved to sing songs.

One of the first things we did was to visit the bar and have a meal. There was a jukebox in there. I was asked to put a con in the jukebox. I chose a Rod Stewart song. We all loved Rod Stewart, even having tartan scarves. The coin dropped in, and everything immediately went dark; the lights went out, and the music stopped. I stood there frozen. There was a lot of laughter coming from somewhere. I realised it was my friends. The manager of the bar disappeared for a minute, then the lights all came back on, and the music started playing.

"Only you could do that." Alan glared at me.

"What do you mean? All I did was as you asked me to do. I put the money in the jukebox, and then the lights went out. How could you say I did that?" I felt angry.

The other guys laughed.

"When you think about it, Rob remarked, still laughing, "if anyone else had put the coin in the jukebox, the lights and fuses would not have blown." To make his point, he went over to the jukebox, chose another song and put a coin in. Nothing happened. Coming back to the table, he sat down with a cheesy grin on his face. "See what I mean? "

I had no idea why. I thought often about being born on the 13th of the month. I thought about everything that had happened to me, how everything I touched seemed to fall apart. Spilling drinks, being blamed for things which happened, even if it appeared I was not there.

The week flew by, and the days were spent surfing or jumping the waves. Namely, the locals called them the Atlantic rollers.

The second week, there was quite a commotion in the campsite. A party if lads arrived. We all recognised them. There was Jim Percy and his pop group, who were currently in the charts, Sham 69!

We played beach volleyball with them. Often beat them and spent some time in the bar, too.

One morning, while I was on the beach, I had yet another clear vision. We were coming back to the camp in Alan's car. As we travelled down a country lane, we stopped at a local pub. Alan noticed a puncture in the front offside tyre. We all got out so the tyre could be changed, only to find there was no jack to lift the car up to change the wheel. We all gathered around the car and, struggling, managed to lift the car up so the tyre could be changed.

I saw another vision. I was getting out of a car and fell over the seat belt, which was quite loose. Somehow, it had not retracted into its holder. As I tripped, the seat belt was tangled around my ankle.

The next day, we decided to go to Truro, just as Josie had told me. As we piled into two cars, I took a deep breath. "I had a premonition last night," I began hesitantly. I waited for my mates to start making rude comments. They usually did when I was going to make a statement.

"What weird dream you have then." One of the boys replied scornfully.

I took another deep breath. "I saw us lifting Alan's car up as he had a puncture in his right front wheel," I replied. "I also saw me getting out of the car, and something went wrong with the seat belt." I finished lamely.

We then set off to Truro and spent some time there buying gifts for our parents. Truro is a city which has quaint little streets and an indoor market in the middle of the city centre. The roads were narrow and mostly cobbled. Little gift shops adorned with crystals, ornaments, crafts and lots of what one would call knick-knacks.

We stopped in a country pub on the way back to the campsite. I began to wonder if what Josie had told me was not going to happen. I think my friend did, too. "Well, nothing has happened so far". One of the boys said. "Maybe your dream was what it was. Just a dream".

We went out into the lane where the cars were parked. As we approached Alan's car, he noticed the front wheel of his car was flat! The boys stared at me. Alan opened the boot of the car and removed the spare tyre. "Darn it, I have no jack to lift the wheel," Alan moaned. "I cannot jack the car up to change the tyre". I stepped forward.

"There are enough of us. Why don't we try and lift the car up, and you change the wheel?" I ventured.

"Flipping Nora! That is a great idea". Lee exclaimed. "For once, Steve has suggested something worthwhile".

We managed to lift the car as Alan changed the wheel. At last, we were on our way.

We arrived back at the camp in the early evening. As we piled out of the cars, I tripped on the seat belt, which was loosely hanging out the door. It tangled up. Thankfully, it was not broken, but it took a bit of sorting out. No matter what we tried, the seatbelt would not retract into its holder. After a while, we just about managed to repair it.

The holiday soon came to an end. We never knew then, but this was the last holiday we would all spend together.

Chapter 9

I am shown my future

One lunchtime, Maralyn, a work colleague, and I decided to go to the pub round the corner to have a meal. We often frequented the pub together. As we left our building, we were discussing meeting someone who we may fall in love with. We often had strange conversations.

I was told by Josie to look up into the clouds, which were racing across the sky. "Look to your left", Josie instructed me. "You will see a name in the clouds". I stopped and looked up. There was a name in the clouds. Linda! "This is a girl you will meet soon, and you will marry her". Josie went on. Then she stood right behind me. "Now look to your right, yes, up there in the clouds". I did as she asked, and I saw a woman in a wooden chair. It looked old-fashioned. It was one of those chairs which had a high back to it. It seemed made of mahogany. Sitting in the chair was a woman with two children sitting on her lap. A boy on one side and a girl on the other. The children looked about 8 and 10. The boy was older. The woman had long dark brown hair and strong cheekbones, which stood out. The boy had dark brown hair like his mum and had her looks, too. The younger girl had light brown hair and seemed a little chubby.

"Who are they?" I asked Josie. "Are they important?"

"The woman you see is called Rosemary. She hates that name and prefers to be called Rose. I am showing you her because in years to come, you will meet this woman and her children". Josie smiled. "Linda, who you will marry, you will meet soon. You will meet her through another girl that you will meet." Josie stepped to my right side. Before I could answer, Josie went away.

I explained what I saw and was told to Maralyn. "Oh my goodness, you are not going to marry Linda"? We both worked with Linda, who I could not get on with. Linda had a love-hate relationship with me. Both of us felt like walking on eggshells. I never knew why, but perhaps we just clashed too many times.

"No way, Maralyn. This is another girl I am going to meet." I stared up at the clouds. Linda was still written in them. "Look up there." I stepped in closer to Maralyn and pointed my finger at the clouds with Linda etched in them. "Can you see Linda there?" Maralyn stared at where I was pointing.

"No, I cannot." Maralyn seemed disappointed. "I do not doubt you, Steve." Then suddenly, Maralyn giggled. "Oh yes! I can now see her name! how odd."

We had a nice meal in the pub. As we walked back to work, a five-minute walk, Maralyn spoke. "You know you can see things, and I know you have a special gift. Can you see a man coming in for me?"

I hesitated. "I do not know. When I get these images or visions, I have no control over what they are about. I believe as we were talking about having boy and girlfriends, I was shown my future". We were now in the car park in front of our workplace. "I do feel you will find true happiness. I think that may be sooner than you think." I do not know why I said this to her. I just felt I had to say something. Deep down, I sensed she would find a guy who would literally sweep her off her feet.

A few months later, the lads and I went out to parties. On one occasion, I briefly spoke to a girl at a party who was with another guy. I could see she was very pretty. Having no confidence in myself, I just sat around sipping a beer. As we left to go home, I had a rough piece of paper shoved into my hand. It had a phone number on it and a short message saying 'ring me.'

"You are in luck," Rob said, laughing. I read the message again.

"Do you know who this message is from?"

"You remember that girl, you know, the one with the reddish brown hair, about five foot two. She was snogging that guy on the sofa. You looked at her when you arrived at the party." I thought deeply about this. The girl in question somehow caught my eye. I remember seeing her. Despite the room being crowded with lots of people, the girl seemed to shine out to me. "Her name is Barbara. I know her. She likes you and I should call her". Rob gave me a knowing wink.

I met up with Barbara a few days later. We dated quite a few times over the next two months. One evening, she took me to an open brethren chapel. I often went to church in St Albans. I was part of the evangelical church. One thing both Barbara and I had in common was we both believed in Jesus.

Barbara then went to university to study psychology in an attempt to get a degree. We unfortunately had to end our relationship.

I decided to go to the church she went to. I was open-minded about religion and felt I wanted to find out more. They often held prayer meetings and a bible class. I met a new friend at this church. I dated a girl from that church, but I knew it was not right. There was another girl who caught my eye. She had red curly hair, a round face and a full body. I noticed she always sat by another girl who was her best friend. I saw they often chatted with each other.

After a few weeks, I really got to know them. Linda, I noticed, had red curly hair, a few freckles on her cheeks, and hazel eyes. We went out many times and, within a year, decided to get engaged.

Eventually, I proposed to Linda. Before I did, Josie came to see me with more news. "You will have three girls with Linda. You will also get divorced." I also remembered Josie telling me I would meet Linda through another girl. That was Barbara.

Dad was a hard-working man. He had a top job in a bank, working in London. We often walked together to the station as this was on the way to my place of work. The wholesaler I worked in was just a five-minute walk from the railway station. "My chest seems worse today", my Dad moaned as we slowly walked to the station. "To be honest, don't tell your Mum; I did not feel like going to work this morning".

"Why don't you go back home and go to the doctor?" I was very concerned.

Suddenly, Josie appeared. "Your Dad will have a heart attack!" she exclaimed. "he will survive but will be in a hospital in London for a while".

I noticed Dad was off-colour. Thinking about what I had just been told, I implored Dad not to go to work. Dad could be stubborn! He gave me a wave and walked into the station.

Later that day, as I walked into the office after having a good day selling lots of paperbacks, Maralyn waved me to her desk. "Your Mum called earlier, around 11 am. Your Dad had a heart attack and is in hospital. She wanted you to go with her and see him".

I stood there frozen. I did not know what to say or do.

"Your brother went with your Mum in the end." Rising from her seat, Maralyn gave me a hug. "I am really sorry; I hope your Dad is not too bad. Maybe it is not as serious as it could be."

When I eventually arrived home, Mum was in the kitchen, fussing around just to be busy. "How is Dad?" I asked tentacular. I was frightened Mum might say he had died. Thoughts of losing my Dad were something I could not bear. What would happen to the house? Would we have to move? How would we all survive, especially Mum, who I knew would not be able to live without him.

Mum turned towards me, tears in her eyes. I could see she was trying to be brave. "Dad is in hospital. He is in a critical condition in ICU," wiping tears from her face, she went into the lounge and sat down in her seat. "The next 24 hours will be very difficult. We shall know if he survives, how it has affected him." Holding a tissue, Mum sniffled into it. "I shall be calling the hospital later to see how he is."

I was nearly crying, too. "I am sorry I missed your call this morning," I could not think of anything else to say. My head was all over the place. "Can I make you a cup of tea?" That was all I thought about asking.

We both sat down, drinking the tea. Mum was in bits. "I would have preferred it if you could have been with me at the hospital". Mum put her cup down on the coffee table. "When we went to see your Dad, John did not walk with me. I wanted someone who would hold my hand. Dad was in an ICU. Wires all over the place". Mum began to cry again. I could feel by the tone of her voice she was upset.

Dad was in hospital for some weeks. Although it was touch and go, he somehow managed to pull through, much to the doctor's amazement. Dad had a massive heart attack. This meant he had to retire early at 48. Although he went back to work part-time, it proved too much for him. Minor attacks made him realise he could never work again.

My parents then discussed selling the house and moving. In between time, Linda and I were planning our wedding and two years following his heart attack, we married in January. It was, in all ways, a white wedding. As we exited the church for the photos, a blizzard arrived and dumped loads of snow on us.

Later that year, Mum, Dad, my younger sister Carol and Kevin, my youngest brother, moved down to Exmouth. Mum and Dad had bought a bungalow in the seaside resort.

I remembered what Josie had told me all those years ago. "Your Mum and Dad will retire in Exmouth. Not everyone will come down. There is a brother, and your baby sister will come down with them. Susan will not, neither will John, but YOU will a few years later."

We often visited my parents, who loved living in Exmouth. Going to the beach, where we went on holiday all those years ago. Memories of when we were younger came back to me. The lovely beach and its rock pools, the tea rooms in the town, where Mum and Dad took us as children, were still there.

Linda gave birth to our first child, a girl. We called her Rachel. I spent a lot of time with her, being jobless and often searching for a decent job.

It was very hard living from hand to mouth. Walking into town to sign on.

Bethan, our second daughter, was born two years later.

One evening, I had a phone call from a sales director for a video game company. "Can you come to my house in St Albans?" he asked me. I went to his house on a Saturday morning. There on his television was a game playing. It was more like a competition than an interview, as we played, but after an hour, he offered me a job. I was so happy the money was good; I got a company car, and I started on Monday. Travelling by train into London and out the other side to a place called Loughton.

I was there for a year before they decided to let the sales force go. Struggling to make ends meet and fearing we would lose our house, we reluctantly put it on the market. One day, my parent rang me up. "Stephen, our friends, gave us an advert for a sales manager's vacancy for a housewares company." Dad gave me the details but warned me, "Don't say you live in Milton Keynes; give them our address." I applied for the vacancy and was soon on the bus to Exmouth to attend the interview.

I was asked to attend another interview in Burnley, where they had their factory and head office. Shortly after, I began working for them. We finally sold our house and bought one in Exmouth. By that time, Linda was heavily pregnant. She gave birth to Aimee just three days after Rachel's 4th Birthday. I remembered what Josie had told me. "You will have three girls with Linda". You will move down to Exmouth a few years after your parents move".

One morning, I had a strange vision. Unlike all the others, this was different.

I was in a flat which, somehow, I knew I owned. I saw myself as much older. The walls were creamy, and the rooms were very bright. Although I was happy, I knew there was no one around me. I was completely on my own. Then, the vision must have moved forward in time. I saw my mother as an old woman lying in a bed. I knew she was going to die of dementia. I saw my father with tears in his eyes as we stood around her bed. There was Carol and

Kevin. I could not see anyone else. Beside stood a lady whom I did not know. She had long dark hair and was quite short in height, around 5 ft.

The vision finished as abruptly as it came. I had no idea what this vision was about. I felt it was something which would maybe materialise sometime. I had no idea how long this would be. I felt it would be a long time. The reason was I did not feel uncomfortable, like in other visions where they happened soon after.

My sales job was a really good vocation. I travelled to Cornwall up to Bristol and across to Hampshire. This meant I had to stay away from home from time to time. It was exciting. Selling housewares and calling on cook shops, wholesalers and farms, too. I found it both enjoyable and tiring. Every few months, we would be asked to attend a sales meeting in Burnley. A five-hour drive. Up the M5 to Birmingham and then the M6 /M65 to Burnley.

I often felt I was not alone when driving. I knew Josie was with me as I travelled around the country.

Chapter 10

My first Circle

I loved living by the sea. From our bathroom window, we could see the sea in the distance. Often, seagulls would nest on the roofs of our houses. Linda worked in a shop in the town, and the girls went to a school just around the corner from where we lived. There was an indoor swimming pool where the girls could go on a Saturday evening to learn to swim. Taking them down to the pool, I eventually was asked if I liked to teach swimming. I jumped at the offer and went on a course, and every Saturday night was filled with me teaching children in the big pool.

One evening, I noticed a young lady sitting on a seat by the side of the pool. She was a parent whom I noticed had two children, a boy and a girl. I had a feeling I knew this lady. 'Where have I seen you before?' I asked myself. She looked familiar and seeing the children I realised where. I approached the lady, remembering the vision and what Josie had told me. This is the woman I saw sitting in a chair having a photo taken with her two children.

"Hello, I am Steve, and I am one of the swimming teachers." I stood by her as she sat on the seat by the pool. "Is your name Rosemary and…."

"I do not like being called Rosemary," she snapped, looking at me. "I prefer Rose." Then, smiling, she apologised. "Sorry, Steve, I did not mean to snap at you." Shuffling on the seat, "How do you know me? Have we met before, goodness me? I don't think we have, except down here." She replied, pointing to the pool.

Of course, I could not tell her I saw her nearly 20 years ago in a vision. I still had no idea why I was shown her by Josie. I made up a story. "Possibly in another life." I joked.

I loved the children I taught to swim. I even went on to coach them in diving. Soon, I became so popular when it was time to move the children up to the next class many left the club. The organisers would contact the parents to ask why the children left. It became clear they loved me teaching them and preferred to leave rather than change teachers. After a while, I was asked to take them back into my class. I was so happy to help these children. I worked with them until they were happy to move up.

I found a Baptist church, which I attended every Sunday. As a family, we went to church, and the girls attended Sunday school. I was asked after a while if I would like to join the music group. We played the songs in the service. Of course, there was an organ and a piano. In the group was a lady who played a tenor recorder; her husband, who was the leader of the group, played the guitar; another guy played base, and from time to time, we had a cellist. I played drums and sometimes a keyboard. Before the main service began, we had praise and being part of the music group, we took turns leading it. This meant standing up in front of the congregation and giving a short message and introduction to the songs. I led this once a month.

After the service, we all gathered in the back room for tea and biscuits. It was a chance for everyone to get to know each other. There was a lady who had two grown-up boys. They were in their 20s. One of them had autism. One morning after the service, this lady approached me. "Stephen, you remind me of Alex, my son. He is autistic. Have you been diagnosed with autism"?

I was taken aback. "No, never," I replied. I was so shocked by this. I thought about those visits to the hospital as a child.

"I have worked with autistic children and adults. I hear you when you speak. Have you noticed if people get confused when you talk to them?" She took me to one side so nobody else could inadvertently overhear our conversation. "You start talking about a subject, then you jump to something which many, including me at first, have no idea what the connection is." She smiled and sipped her cup of tea. "For example, say we are talking about the beach. I notice we talk about the beach, and then you talk about something which seemingly has nothing to do with the beach. After a while, you come back to the main conversation." She began to laugh. "It is quite funny, but it is not really."

"Mum was told by a consultant when I was very young I had what he described as a grasshopper brain. I go from one subject to another and back in a great big circle."

"Having the experience of a parent with an autistic son and seeing other children and adults with the condition, I must say you definitely fall into the bracket. I have been watching you for months, Stephen." I was surprised. "I study people. You are a genius being able to do the things you can, like teaching yourself how to drum and play the keyboard and play by ear."

I have never thought of myself as being gifted. Being shot down in flames so often does knock one's confidence.

Many times later in my life, people who studied Psychology would approach me and say when they had studied autism, they thought of me.

I began to realise why I was different. Not just being able to see Angels.

In the middle of the town was Moose Hall. A Spiritualist church. I had never been to one before. My friends took me down there one Sunday evening. It was quite crowded in there. Seats were put out in rows with an aisle down the middle. A lady stood in the front and asked us to give a warm welcome to a visiting medium. I sat there wondering what this was all about. Honestly, I have never gone to a Spiritualist church before.

"The medium connects to your loved ones in heaven." Someone whispered.

The medium was a jolly little lady. She wore a white scarf and a purple dress. She was only about 5ft 4" tall. She was it seems very good! Not seeing this before, I was impressed with her. She not only described the said person but also gave out messages. "You have lost your keys in your kitchen"" she announced to a friend of mine. "They disappeared two years ago. They will come back in three years". My friend gasped. She had lost her keys; they were last seen on the kitchen table.

From the church, I met a lady who was starting a beginner's Circle in her house. I asked to join, and she took me in. The house was just literally across the road from us. Leaving our house, I walked down our road to some steps which led to a main road. Crossing the road, her house was just a few yards away. The Circle was on a Monday evening. It started at 7pm and was supposed to finish at 8.30. The lady who ran the Circle, Annie, was quite well-built and always had a smile on her face.

"Who is that girl on the stairs?" I asked her as I entered her home. This was the first week.

Wiping her hands on a tea towel, Annie gave me a shocked look. "You can see a girl on my stairs?" She asked, very surprised. "Can you describe her?"

I stared at the girl on the stairs. "She is sitting on the third stair going up. Has mousey brown hair with riglets down just past her shoulders, wearing a red gingham frock, and is holding a doll with blonde hair. The girl is combing her dolly hair. She looks about 7 years old". I finished.

"Oh my goodness, you are very good, Stephen. That little girl has been on that stair for a few years. I can see her, and you have described her exactly."

There was a knock on the door, and some more people came in. All girls, I noticed. I was the only guy there.

We soon began the Circle. Not before Annie had told them about what I had seen. "I think Stephen has been in a circle before". She finished. I told her and all the others I had never sat in a circle.

The Circle consisted of two 20-minute meditations. That was all. Every week, we did the same thing. When we began the meditation, I saw nothing but black then colours. The others saw castles, horses, and lots of things. I felt quite disappointed.

"You will improve eventually". Annie comforted me after. "Most people do not get much, not even colours at first".

I persevered and soon found things were getting better. I found myself finding myself above the table, looking down at all of us around it from the ceiling. I had no idea what was going on as I slipped into meditation. From the ceiling, I dipped down, and I did not know what happened after. This happened every week. One week, we were asked, as we often were, what we saw in our meditations.

All of the others began to get a common theme. "Stephen was in our meditation". They exclaimed.

I sat there mystified. I explained that I went on my journey and told them what I saw. How could I be in their meditations?

One week, I found the reason.

The girl who sat on the stairs was taking me up to the ceiling, where I could see the others sitting around the table. Then, she took me into their meditations. How did I find out?

The girl spoke. "My name is Elizabeth. I take you on your journey". Later, I found out she was my elder sister in a past life. In Victorian times. I was just 4 years old, and she was 8 years old when I had diphtheria and died. I also found out why she was at Annie's house. She was waiting for me!

I still wonder how Elizabeth knew I would turn up at Annie's house.

After a year of attending the Circle, Annie told me to leave. I had no real explanation as to why, but I think my exploits with Elizabeth had a lot to do with it. I did hear, many years later, that she disappeared from Annie's house very soon after I left the Circle.

I never attended another circle again!

Moose Hall became a regular Sunday evening venue. Often, the visiting medium would ask if anyone knew a Robert, Roger, Richard, John, Margaret, Mary, you get the drift. We were asked to put our hands up if we could take a name, and then the description followed. If anyone could not take this, then our hands were lowered. There was one family who stuck their hands up and took everything. So they always had a message. Often, we would groan as they seemed to have a problem lowering their hands. They were eventually labelled as 'Message stealers.'

A medium came one Sunday; she had grey hair and was dressed in a nice flowery dress. She wore light-rimmed glasses. As she worked the room, she eventually came to me. "You young man. You should be up here doing this. Why aren't you?" I did not know what to say. "You are reading a book about the Dalai Mala." she continued.

Indeed, I was actually reading the book and wondered how she knew. I was stuck on Chapter 5 at the time, where the Dalai Mala was outside the city sitting on the ground. "You are stuck on Chapter 5". The medium smiled at me. I gasped in surprise. Acknowledging her, she moved on. That message was the first one I can remember having in a Spiritualist church!

One week, we had a medium coming from Wiltshire. He was happy to do one-to-one readings for anyone who wanted them on a Saturday afternoon and Sunday morning. They were to be recorded if anyone wanted this. I booked a reading for Saturday. I went to the hall up the side stairs to a room where the medium was sitting at a table. I noticed he had broken teeth and long hair tied into a ponytail. His attire was adorned with lots of necklaces around him, which looked like old bones. "Do you want this recorded?" he asked me. I noticed his London accent. I told him I did, and he put the tape into the machine.

After he shuffled his cards, he handed them to me to shuffle. "Take 7 out". I did as he asked and put them on the table as he requested. Just before he began, he pressed the buttons on the machine for it to record.

Within a flash, Josie appeared next to me. "Tell him the recorder will not record your reading, and every reading he will do and has done will not be recorded."

I passed on the message. The medium gave me a scornful look and double-checked the recorder. Stopping the recording, he pointed to it. "Look at this: I press play and record, both at the same time and you can see the tape going round."

I had the reading and paid him the money for the recording, too. I saw my brother and a few other people later and told them the medium readings would not be on tape. I do not think anyone actually believed me.

The next evening, the medium was doing platform. He looked quite sorry for himself. The chair lady made an announcement. "Before the medium begins his clairvoyance, he wishes to apologise to everyone who paid extra to have their reading recorded. Unfortunately, the recordings did not come out. If you see me after, I shall reimburse you the money."

Kevin was sitting in the aisle opposite. I glanced at him. He nodded his head, acknowledging me.

The church was always busy, so it was a good idea to go down early to get a seat. Sometimes, Dad would come with us, and Carol often accompanied him. I seldom had a message, but I did not mind. I knew if something important was to be heard, then I would get a message.

One day, Kevin came round to our house. He and his family lived literally around the corner. On this occasion, Kevin was standing at the top of my drive, which sloped down to my garage, where my car was. "There is a native red Indian standing by you," I said, pointing to his left. Kevin just stood there.

"Okay."

"He has one feather in his headdress, and he is 12 years old. He has a tomahawk in his right hand. He tells me he will spend the next year with you, just one year, then he will go. He is here to learn from you." I finished with a smile.

Kevin looked at me in disbelief. "Okay, thank you". That is all he said. I had a distinct impression that Kevin did not believe me.

Exactly one year later, a medium gave Kevin a message. I was sitting adjacent to him. The main aisle separated us. "You have a young red Indian boy with you," the medium told Kevin. "He has been with you for a year. He has a tomahawk in his right hand, and he tells me it is time for him to leave."

Chapter 11.

I met Trish.

I loved my job as a sales representative. Selling housewares and agricultural products was both exciting and challenging. Staying in hotels was okay once I found nice ones which I regularly stayed in.

One day, I was visiting an agricultural customer in Calne. The buyer was a nice, gentle guy. Black hair, cut to short back and sides, Black rimmed spectacles and even a dark, almost black suit. He was slightly shorter in height than me. We had it seems a lot in common. He believed in Jesus, and often, we would talk about how Jesus lives within us. I lead worship from time to time in my Baptist church. He always carried with him a bible. During the time he was giving me a nice order, he would suddenly open his bible and spout scripture. I did not mind too much, but sometimes it was a little overwhelming.

On another occasion, when visiting, I told him I needed to call my wife, Linda. "Can I borrow your phone?" I asked politely. He passed the phone to me.

"Dial 0 first, then the number. I did and heard the phone in the house ringing.

"Hello," Linda's voice squeaked down the line.

I replied, "It's me, Steve. You have a letter for me in a brown envelope. It came this morning."

I heard shuffling noises. "Yes, I have a letter here for you. How did you know this?" Linda was quite taken aback.

"I want you to open it," I said. I heard her open the letter, and when she was ready, I went on to read the letter out.

Linda was shocked. "How can you be miles away and read the letter like you did?"

Meanwhile, the buyer, who was in earshot, was staring at me. I finished the call and turned toward the buyer. He held his bible up in front of his face. "You are a devil!" he called out to me. "How you can do what you have done is beyond belief".

I explained to him calmly. "You know I work with Jesus? Well, it was Jesus who told me to call my wife, and he showed me the letter". I could see the puzzlement on the buyer's face. There was he, studying the bible 24/7 and me, just an ordinary guy, actually hearing Jesus speak to me?

After that visit, he was quite different when he saw me. He had his bible, which he always had in his hands. However, I found he was more respectful if one can say that, about my spirituality. We became much closer in being friends.

I was in Torquay. I had an overdraft, and it was coming to an end. If I wanted to extend the time, I needed to phone my bank. I rang my bank. I gave them the reference and details or most of them as far as I could.

"Have you got the letter on you?" The young lady asked me.

"No, I haven't. I am out on the road and in a phone box." I replied.

"Can you hold on for a minute?" I did, and a few minutes later, she was back. "I have just gone down to the office, and I do not know how you have these details because the letter is being typed up to be sent to you as we speak." A pause. "The reference you gave us is in the letter. How come you have these details when the letter has not been posted?" I felt her concern and confusion.

All I could say was somehow I could see the letter.

Two days later, the letter arrived in the post. The details were exactly as I told her on the phone.

On another day, I was in Bristol to call on a wholesaler. Josie appeared in the passenger seat. She is sitting there with a huge Cheshire cat smile on her face. I was taken by surprise. This was the first time I had seen Josie in my car. "You need to call on Kitchens in Whiteladies Road. They have been sent the wrong bun tins. They ordered plain ones, and they received 48 fancy ones." Josie stared out the window at the scenery.

I parked my car as near as I could to the kitchens, as it was a busy street. I found a place nearly opposite.

"Good morning. I know I am not due to call on you, but I understand you have received 48 bun tins, which were not the correct ones." I said cheerfully to the assistant behind the counter. Josie stood by me.

She went downstairs. A few minutes later, she reappeared with a confused and puzzled look on her face. "I have just asked the girls downstairs, and they tell me the delivery has just been made. Yes, we have realised your company sent us the wrong bun tins." Leaning over the counter, "How did you know we had the wrong delivery? We have not rung your company to advise them yet."

Josie grabbed my attention. "Just tell them you knew". She softly advised me.

"I just had a feeling," I replied.

I collected the bun tins and left the shop. Next time, on a regular visit, a few weeks later, they were still talking about this episode.

Saturday evenings, we went to the swimming baths as usual. I met many families whose children came into my class. One particular family were Dave and Frederike. They brought their eldest of three girls to me for her first lesson in the big pool. We eventually became good friends. Frederike, a Dutch lady, spoke both English and her native language. Our families often went to parties. It turned out Frederike was in hospital giving birth to one of her girls, when our neighbour Nicky was in at the same time, giving birth to her second child.

Dave and Frederike were having a party, and we were all invited to it. There was some of her family from Holland there. It was a really fun afternoon. I met Marianne, Frederike's sister. Marianne also lived in Exmouth. She was very tall. 6ft 1. Made me feel like a dwarf, standing next to her. She had mid-length, straight, light brown hair and always had a good story to tell.

We became good friends.

Marianne was interested in 'psychic stuff'. So, we both met up on a Sunday evening and went to Moose Hall.

One evening, we were all informed that there was a special workshop taking place. Spiritual healing with Trish Doherty. We both signed up for it.

Trish lived in a small village in Somerset. The healing workshops mainly took place in her house. Trish always gave a warm welcome. She had blonde, light brown hair, always laughing, and we took to each other virtually straight away. My brother Kevin turned up.

"I would not have Stephen in your group," Kevin announced as he entered the front door. "He is a loose cannon, and he will be a nuisance and cause trouble."

Before I could say anything, Trish stopped him in his tracks. "I run this show, and I decide who comes and goes!" Trish was quite stern. "If Stephen does cause a problem, then I will decide. If you cause trouble or anyone in this group, I shall make the decisions, who stays or goes, not you!"

There were around 16 of us. I was outnumbered, as I was virtually the only boy in the group. Trish had us all introduce ourselves and tell her what we hoped to achieve. We all made little speeches. "I would like to be a good healer and help others". I explained when it came to my turn.

The course ran for several weeks, every two weeks. At last, after what seemed a very long time, the exam came. There were two strange ladies whom we did not know. We each took turns 'scanning' one of the women sitting in the chair and reporting to Trish what we found. I was really nervous.

Trish pulled me to one side, taking me into her kitchen. "You are really good, Stephen. Don't doubt yourself." Following her back into the main room, I began my session.

Ten minutes later, I reported to Trish. She beamed in my direction. "Well done." Then to everyone. "Congratulations to you all."

I was so happy! I now could say to everyone, 'I am a Spiritual healer'.

Some of us continued to go to Trish's house to learn other things. Reading tarot, flowers, handprints in the sand, and seeing auras. Marianne came with me most of the time. The girls would, with Trish encouraging them to pick on me. One time, we all asked to bring flowers along. Not to tell anyone which flower you brought with you. They were all put tidily on a board, and we sat in chairs in the main room. Trish told me to wait in the kitchen until I was called in. I was going to be first.

I was eventually called in. Everyone sat there in a semi-circle, waiting with smirks on their faces. I picked up a flower. 'How am I going to read this?' I asked myself. Trish told me to relax and focus on the plant, the stem, the leaves and say whatever comes. After a few minutes of staring at the flower, I began. Trish smiled a knowing smile. I began to grow in confidence and came out with lots of stuff which I could not understand nor make sense. I finished.

"Now, who does this flower belong to?" Trish. Asked me. Encouraging me to take a moment to work this out. Finally, I pointed to a lady. Trish laughed as the lady shook her head. It was not hers. It was the lady sitting bang next door to her. I received a huge clap, and we all took turns.

On another occasion, Trish brought in a sand pit. We all sat in our chairs as Tris explained what we were going to do. Each, in turn, would put our hand in the sand to leave a print. The person who was not in the room when we did this was to come in and read the print, then say whose it was.

I was then ushered out into the kitchen. Trish always made me go first. But although it was hard, I joined in the fun of the sessions.

I came back into the room. I noticed the girls were giggling. I looked deep into the sand, saying what I was being told. It was not easy, to say the least. I told Trish what I saw and felt, then came the difficult part. Whose is it? Slowly, I looked around the room at the girls in the chairs. I pointed to one. A hit! I was right. Now, the pressure was on the others. Trish put her arm around me. "I knew you could do it."

Trish and I became really close friends. Often, she would encourage me to learn to see auras, read tarot and even do mediumship. The others all joined in, and we all had so much fun and laughter. One afternoon, Trish had a couch set up in the living room. "We are all going to practice Spiritual healing in a different way to what we did on the course." Trish brought out a lot of crystals. On her directions, we placed them under the couch. One of the girls was asked to lie down on the couch. We were placed all around the couch, one at each end and all of us around the side. "Place your hands near but not touching the patient and see what you feel," Trish instructed us. We did as she asked. Suddenly, I thought I saw blue lightning coming from my fingers and touching the girl on the couch. It was only for a few seconds.

"Did you see that?" one of the girls exclaimed, staring at me. "Stephen had lightning coming out of his fingertips."

The other girls stopped. Trish stared at me. "I saw the lightning, although it was only for a few seconds". Trish began to laugh. "In all my days, I have never seen that happen before!"

Everyone looked at me. I felt embarrassed. They all saw it. Some said they saw a flash. We carried on taking turns on the couch. The lightning did not come again. I felt the others were disappointed.

Being virtually the only guy in the group, I found very quickly that for anything new we tried, I was the one who was the guinea pig.

One time, Trish asked me to accompany her as she was doing clairvoyance in Yeovil. "You can draw auras, and I shall do the clairvoyance," she explained.

When we were on our way, I noticed Josie was with us. "Tell Trish the chairs in the church are separated down the middle". Josie held my hand. I repeated what Josie had told me to Trish.

"How do you know?" Trish replied as she navigated a roundabout. I noticed a helicopter cut out from the greenery in the middle of it. "Have you been to this church before?"

I told her I had never been here, and I just knew.

We parked in the car park and walked into the church, which had a glass-fronted door. Inside, there was an aisle down the middle of the chairs. On the far right in the corner was a plinth where the speaker would stand when giving a sermon. "That is where you will be, drawing your auras," Trish told me. "Let's go into the kitchen and put the kettle on." The kitchen was out the back of the building.

Trish was helping set the place up when Josie appeared again. She had a beaming smile on her face. "Stephen, a lady with reddish hair is coming to this church. She has brown horse-rimmed spectacles, and she is wearing a green top. Follow me," Josie walked out into the main hall. "See that chair," Josie pointed to a seat on the right, two seats from the aisle and the second row from the front. "The lady who I am talking about will sit here."

I went up to Trish and told her what Josie had told me. Then, back in the kitchen, I began to make the tea. The kettle had just boiled. I picked up a tin of biscuits to put them on a plate.

"Stephen, come here!" Trish called me from the main hall in a loud whisper. "That lady you mentioned, is this her?"

I was so surprised I dropped the tin of biscuits I held in my hand. Rushing out to the front of the church, I saw a lady walk slowly in. Just as Josie had described! Trish was excited. The lady strolled to the second row and sat in the seat I had pointed out. Trish rushed me into the kitchen.

"I do not know how you know this, Stephen; you really do have a special gift."

The evening began a short while later. Trish was passing messages from loved ones in spirit. I was busy drawing guides and auras. I was not that good at drawing faces, but I loved drawing the auras which I could see. Trish was going around the room at one point, asking if I was ready. I said I was.

"I have this picture of a guide who seems to have a flat head." I began, lifting the picture so the audience could see it. I was speaking to a woman in the back of the church. The picture showed a flat line and a face drawn with colours of the lady's aura around it. Explaining the colours, the lady gasped. "My guide looks exactly like that," she exclaimed excitedly. "He comes from a tribe who are flat-headed people."

Trish smiled and then went on to send another message.

Meanwhile, I was drawn to the lady who Josie had seen coming in earlier.

"You have a connection to a North American Indian Cheyanne tribe through a marriage." I ventured slowly. "She is a medicine lady who worked with herbs, and this connection has a lady who does this." I went on, finishing with her aura.

The lady smiled warmly. "My son Robert is married to a young girl who comes from that tribe; she works with natural remedies, using herbs and flowers."

"Wow!" a lot of people in the audience exclaimed. Trish was really happy.

"Stephen may not be able to draw faces very well, but I must say he can do a good picture of a guide." She turned to me and clapped. Everyone in the church gave me a resounding clap.

For the very first time, I felt good about myself. I was so used to being bullied that having people clap me was a new experience.

After this experience, Trish encouraged me to believe in myself. On another occasion, we, as her fledglings, went to many churches and practised our mediumship. One evening, in another church in Yeovil. There were six of us. Trish introduced us and told everyone they were in for a treat. I had acute tennis elbow at the time. The pain was really bad, and I found it hard to focus. I sat there as the other fledglings had a go. Then Trish called me out. I stood up feeling very nervous. "Stephen has tennis Elbow and has a lot of pain, so can you all support him, please?" I looked at Trish and saw a big smile on her face. "Stephen is very good and funny, too; you are in for a treat."

My nerves jangled. I looked around the room, and at the back, two girls were standing together. It was crowded in the hall, so no more chairs were available. I saw a rainbow above them. Taking a deep breath, I began to do an impression of the characters in the television program named Rainbow. Everyone laughed! I gave them the message, and they took it. I felt relieved. I had managed to pass on a message despite the pain.

Trish stood up. "I did warn you, Stephen, despite the pain in his elbow, is so funny and special." She turned to me. "I think it best you should sit out this next session, Stephen."

I was in pain.

The others had another go and I sat there listening to them, they were good! As I sat there, I was drawn to a young lady sitting in the front. I saw her grandma leaning over her. She held a large apple pie with sugar dusted on the top. She was a large, round woman with grey curly hair.

Eventually, the others finished their turns, and the proceedings came to an end. Time for everyone to mingle and have a cup of tea or coffee cakes and biscuits. The girl whose grandma was with me came over to me.

"I noticed you were staring at me," she began. "I reckon, if you had another chance, you may have come to me?"

We both sat down with our drinks. She had reddish brown hair and a few freckles on her cheeks, I noticed. Hazel eyes, a warm complexion. I told her what I saw. She beamed at me.

"Yes, that was my grandmother. She always baked an apple pie."

I went on to tell her lots of things. "You are planning to go on a trip to Australia. Taking a year out from Uni". I began. "Your grandmother is telling me you have a very mischievous brother who gets into trouble". The young girl laughed.

"You are really good at this. I have never had such a good message in all my days."

Now, it was my turn to smile.

The two ladies who were at the back of the church spoke to me after. They told me how funny I was and praised me for the message. "You are so different. "They remarked.

Soon, it was time to go, and we left.

At another time, Trish asked us to try an exercise. "I would like you to all pair up and sit facing each other. Now take each other's hands and just hold them." We chose who we wished to pair up with. I was one of the girls. "Now, choose who is going first," Trish instructed us. Kevin decided he would. "The one who goes first is in charge. The other partner needs to just relax, close your eyes and empty any thoughts you may have. Just .... relax.... close your eyes... and relax." Trish repeated more slowly. "The one in charge, close your eyes and relax. Try to focus on your colleague and see if you get anything. A picture.... A thought.... A word.... Anything."

We all took it in turns. When it was time for me to see what I picked up, it amazed me. We tried the exercise again; this time, we had to see if we could pick up a past life and send it to the other person.

I was shocked as I was sent a vision. "The visions are yours." Trish told us, "Not the person who is sending it to you".

I saw myself on a train entering a station. As it came into the town, I noticed over the railway was an arch which had writing in German. 'Welcome to Auschwitz'

When the exercise was over, I was in a daze. Trish picked up a glass of water and told me to take a sip. "Did you see anything, Stephen?" Trish sat down. I explained what I saw. The others in the group were astonished. Although they had seen things, my reaction was overwhelming.

Later, I began to remember what Josie had told me all those years ago about the nightmares and what they meant. Why I had taken so much interest in the Holocaust. Why I had read so many books about the Jews in concentration camps during the war.

Slowly, it dawned on me why. The reason is because I was there.

Trish became a bigger part of my life. I did not know this at the time, but we would become very close friends.

Sooner than I thought, everything would become crystal clear to me. I began to see my previous life in Auschwitz in more detail.

That is for another day.

Chapter 12

Sarah

It was nearing my 36th birthday. We often walked around to see my parents, who lived in their bungalow half a mile from us. 600 yards as the crow flies. Mum would put a spread out for us. Cakes, biscuits, sandwiches, tea or coffee. Dad would be sitting in his armchair, often with a smile on his face. They had a large garden, which was mainly grass. A patio in the back garden, where he had a BBQ. It was all open plan, which meant one could just walk from the front garden around the side of the bungalow to the back garden. Mum loved her roses, and there were a few rose bushes spread out around the garden.

Around my birthday, there was going to be a family gathering. A distant relative was due to visit my parents. They were travelling all the way from Derbyshire.

I was getting worried as I was nearing my birthday. I had never forgotten what Josie had told me when I was 19 years of age. "Just before your 36th birthday, you will die."

I had told Linda, my wife, and my children and reminded my parents of this. "Don't be silly". My Mother exclaimed. "That is nonsense; you know you are not going to die. I do not wish to hear you talking rubbish". That was the end of it as far as my Mum was concerned.

A week or so later, I had a fallout with my sister Carol. It was a mountain out of a molehill situation. I had stood my ground.

Two weeks before my birthday, I received a letter from Carol. I sat down to open it and read the contents. It was not a nice letter at all. Telling me what she thought of me; the final sentence was, 'You are dead!'

I put the letter down, shaking with anger. All that was written in the letter was not entirely true. Everything had been thrown out of context. I was really annoyed.

Suddenly, Josie appeared and sat down next to me. "This is what I warned you about when you were just 19!" Josie placed her hands on my wet cheeks and made me look at her. "This letter is what I saw, but I could not tell you at the time. You have 'died' as I told you. She gave me a hug. "This is a new beginning for you".

I smiled in relief and then laughed. Linda came into the lounge. "What is funny?" she inquired.

I told her what Josie had told me. "You know I always said I would die two weeks before my 36th birthday?" I began, showing her the letter. I pointed to the last line. 'You are dead'. "This is what it is all about. "I am dead, but not dead if you get the meaning". I felt so happy. For years, I had dreaded this time, believing my life would end for real. Our children growing up with no dad, my wife being a young widow.

We walked round to see my parents. I showed them the letter. "You see, I did die before my 36th birthday, after all". I pointed out. I was so relieved, I think my parents were too, but they were not happy with Carol. "I know this is a shock", I went on, "but look on the bright side; I have a future to look forward to".

My birthday came and went, and soon all was forgotten. Carol and I had a chat, me reminding her of the prediction that I would die before my 36th birthday and how she played a part in it. We both laughed in the end. Carol and I became very close after this. I think we understood each other much better than ever before.

In Exmouth, there was a local Sea cadets, which my girls decided to join. Linda went with them. They met every week on a certain evening, and once a year, they went on a weekend sprint to Plymouth, where all the Sea Cadets from all over the Southwest met. They called it 'away days. ' Linda and the girls went down on a minibus. I had a nice weekend on my own.

It was on these weekends that my girls met new friends.

A young girl with light brown mousey-coloured hair, hazel eyes, became friends with Bethan. Sarah was funny and full of beans. Her family lived in Teignmouth, and sometimes we went to visit her Mum and family.

Sarah loved being in the Sea cadets and also was quite interested in 'Spiritual stuff'.

I remember visiting her in the hospital as Bethan became very close to her.

Sarah came to visit us one weekend to stay over. I was meditating, and my gatekeeper appeared. He is a Tibetan monk, and he has been with me for years. I asked him if I could have his name, and he told me it was about time I did. "Bee". He spoke in a soft voice.

I could not get the rest. Sarah came upstairs, and I asked her if she could help me. Together, we concentrated. "bee ------ harr," I whispered.

Sarah giggled. Focussing really hard, "Shee harrr", Sarah exclaimed.

We both laughed. "Bee shee harrr. That is his name". Just to make sure I focussed on my gatekeeper. He smiled and acknowledged that this was his name.

One day, I was travelling down to Cornwall, as my sales job took me there. As I drove down the A30 I noticed a man sitting next to me. "Who are you?" I asked. I was not too surprised these days, as many times, people would pop up from nowhere and talk to me. I noticed he wore a grey crew neck pullover, a white shirt and a coloured tie. His hair was salt and pepper grey, cut very short. It was almost a crew cut. He had a round face and brown eyes. He sat there smiling as I drove. "I love Cornwall," he began. "My name is Arthur. I am Sarah's uncle".

I thought about that one. I think 'Arthur' read my thoughts. "Your daughter is friends with my niece. I am talking about Sarah Riley, whom you know". He shuffled in the seat. "You met Sarah in the hospital when she was a patient".

"Oh yes, I recall that". I replied. She is a very lovely friend to Bethan". I replied.

"Can I join you for a while? I have not been down this way for years," Arthur relaxed in his seat, reached into a bag, which suddenly materialised, brought out a newspaper and began to read it; I could not refuse him, so I agreed.

When I next saw Sarah, she giggled when I told her about Arthur. "That was my uncle." Sarah was still laughing. "He nearly always wore that jumper, and he loved Cornwall. I wonder why he decided to go with you." I was not sure if that was a question. I thought about it for a minute.

"Possibly because I can see spirit, and he is your relative; he came to me knowing I can see him."

Often, when I was in company, spirits would suddenly appear.

We had a lot of fun on that day, often practising tarot readings, dowsing, and enjoying the experience.

Sarah still lives in South Devon. She has a lovely family and is very much in touch with us.

Chapter 13

I met Saint Peter.

I was approaching my 40th birthday.

I remember my dad when he was 40, and he told us, "Life begins at 40".

My biggest customers were Trago Mills. They had three stores, one in Newton Abbot, which was a huge store with outlets attached. One little store in Falmouth at the edge of town and the main branch in Liskeard, where the buying office was. I went to see the buyer, a lovely guy called David, who everyone in my company who met him told me he looked like me. David and I became very close, and when I visited him, we often went out for a meal before we did business.

My job was to count the stock, both in the store and in the warehouses, which was a task in itself.

I was counting the stock in the Newton Abbot branch. When I had completed my count, I was drawn to one of the outlet shops, which was independent of Trago Mills. In the window of one of these shops, I saw a lovely crystal ball. I stared at it through the window. Feeling a cold shiver, I knew Josie had appeared. "Go in and buy it". She encouraged me.

I stepped inside the shop. It was small inside but filled with crystals, incense, dream catchers, and tarot cards. I wondered why I had not 'seen' this shop before. I had been walking past this place many times since I began to work for this company, but for some reason, although these shops had been there, today was the first time I saw this one. Soft, dreamy music hummed inside, and I felt at home.

"Can I help you?" the owner asked. I noticed she was dressed in a purple dress and had bangled on her wrists of all different colours. She had wavy dark reddish-brown hair, a beaming smile and eyes which seemed very dark brown. I noticed she wore a number of necklaces.

"I am interested in the crystal ball you have in your window." I cleared my throat.

The lady went to the window and carefully lifted the crystal ball from its display. Placing it on the display counter, she invited me to inspect it. The crystal ball had a clear crystal, and immediately, I knew I had to buy it. I noticed the price. £40. I thought to myself 'This is a bargain."

I bought the crystal ball.

I do not know why I did, but I knew it was important to buy it. Josie laughed and jumped up and down with excitement. I asked her why she was so happy. "You wait and see." She giggled.

My dad's mother, who I never met as she died before I was born, used to scry the crystal ball. Dad often told us how he watched her do readings in the kitchen as he grew up. "Mum used to always start with the past, then the present, then finish with the future," he would tell us very proudly as he remembered those halcyon days. "Often the client who she was reading forgot up in the middle of the reading and walked away," Dad smiled wickedly. "My mother was so accurate; they could not take the future, so they left. Mind you, they paid her." He added as an afterthought.

Dad had kept her crystal ball. When he showed it to us one time, I noticed how clear it had been, though over the years it had become, it seemed quite dull. There was a scratch on the crystal. "Slight damage to it," Dad explained. I remember telling Dad that I was interested in scrying a crystal ball. Eventually, he decided to pass it on. I fervently hoped I would get it, but sadly, I did not! Dad felt it best to pass it to Kevin, my youngest brother. I was very happy for Kevin, although I could not see him ever using the crystal ball, which made my disappointment harder to bear.

I was happy to show off my crystal ball. I had no real idea how to scry it. I practised hard, peering into the ball and feeling disappointed I could not see anything.

One day, I took it around my friend's house. "What a lovely crystal ball." Frederike stared at it. "Can you see anything in it?"

I placed the crystal ball on a coffee table. It was quite heavy; I noticed about 60 cm in diameter. I sat in the stand.

Frederike sat opposite me. "Go on, Steve, give it a try," she encouraged me.

I leaned over the ball and stared into it. After a few minutes, I thought I saw something.

"I can see oranges," I said quite excitedly. "Do you like them?" I sat back with a huge smile on my face.

Frederike smiled and then pointed to the coffee table. There beside the crystal ball was a bowl of oranges.

I decided to give up. Placing the ball back inside the box, I put it away.

It was some years later I pulled it out again.

I was still going to the local Baptist church in Exmouth. Being part of the music group, I loved sitting up in front of the church, in a corner, getting a good view of the minister and organist.

One particular Sunday, I was watching the minister preaching as he usually did. All at once, a man appeared standing next to him. He wore a long white wrap cloak, just like the disciples wore. I noticed he was smiling at me. "You can see me then!" I was not sure if he was asking or telling me. "Yes," I replied. "I can see you. Who are you?"

I am one of the disciples. Have a guess which disciple I am." He teased.

I stared at him. He had dark brown hair. I noticed he had a large nose. His face was covered in a beard. "Give me a clue."

He frowned and then laughed. "I denied Jesus three times."

Immediately, I knew who this man was. "St Peter!" I exclaimed.

St. Peter clapped his hands. Then he picked up a leaflet from the pulpit, which was out of sight from the congregation. "He has forgotten to read this," St. Peter held the leaflet up so I could see it. Then, turning toward the minister, who was still talking to us, he waved it in front of him. "Oy! You have forgotten to read this." Then he put the leaflet down, and with a wink, St Peter stepped down from the pulpit and strolled out of the church. "See you at the pearly gates," he called out to me as he left.

A minute later, the minister stopped talking and reached down to his left where the leaflet was. Picking it up, he held it up. "I forgot to read this out".

In the meantime, I was relating all this in real-time, whispering to the pianist who sat next to me. When the service was over, we all congregated in the back room to have our usual drinks and biscuits. Rosie, the pianist, announced to everyone what I had related to her. The looks of astonishment could be felt.

Any doubts were stifled as Rosie explained the leaflet and how I saw it before the rest of us.

Seeing St Peter was a shock! It was quite unexpected, and I felt blessed I could see and talk to him.

I know Josie was always looking out for me. I often knew she was around me, even if she did not speak. Knowing she was with me often gave me comfort, even in my darkest hours.

I was parked in a county lane, having my lunch one day. It was a pleasant day, sunny and rather warm. As I sat there eating my lunch, I noticed a change. I was no longer sitting behind the wheel of my car. I saw a man in a green and light creamy coloured uniform reaching over me, showing me dials and telling me how to fly a plane. I looked around and saw myself on a runway at an airport. The man was showing me how to turn the wheel gently. "Pull it towards you, and you will rise up," He was smiling, encouraging me to follow his instructions. I was sitting in a two-seater plane which had two wings.

The next instant, I was back in my car. This was a surreal vision. I felt I was in it rather than just viewing it. A new way of 'seeing'.

A few days later, Linda and I were both sitting up in bed. "I have a really nice 40th birthday present for you." Linda laughed. "I bet in a month of Sundays, you will never guess what I have bought you," I turned to look at her. Linda's face was beaming, and I felt her excitement bubbling away. "Go on, have as many guesses as you like, but I know you will never get it right."

I knew she would keep me awake. The excitement was electric.

I relaxed and began to tell her my vision. I noticed Linda was sitting there with a face of incredibility. "I reckon you have bought me a ticket so I can fly a plane. A first world war plane." I finished, remembering the type of plane I saw myself sitting in. "Is this what you have brought me?"

Linda slowly reached into the drawer of the bedside cabinet next to her. We had one on each side of the bed.

Passing me a pamphlet, I noticed all the excitement had drained from her. "I can never keep a secret from you." Passing me the pamphlet.

I opened it up and read the legend. There was a picture of a First World War plane and a ticket for me to go to the airport and fly in one, actually flying it for a minute or two.

Due to weather conditions, I was not able to take the flight until the spring of the following year. It was an amazing experience. Just as I was shown in my vision. I sat in the back seat of the open-roofed plane and had a go flying it.

I often felt unhappy, even depressed, which affected my mental health. I was still being made fun of and the joker in the family. Many times, I would feel like I did not belong and wished I could go to sleep and never wake up.

Coming back home one evening, I decided to go to Haldon Hill, just outside Exeter. There were some lovely woods to walk in. There were several areas where you could park your car and take your pet for a walk or just stroll through the woods. It was a very beautiful place. This particular evening, I drove into the woods and parked my car in a secluded spot. I made sure that there was no one else nearby. I decided to gas myself and end it all. I had the radio on as the car filled up with smoke. Me.

I have no idea how long I was in my car. Suddenly I heard the radio, different songs and a new presenter. The car was clearing of smoke. I honestly thought I was in Heaven. Slowly getting out of the car, the thought of being in Heaven was confounded as I was met by five or six Angels standing by the car. They all smiled at me. "Am I in Heaven?" I asked them.

"No, you are not! We have other plans for you, and one of them is not to take you up to Heaven."

Immediately, I swore at them. I was annoyed, very angry. I called them all the names under the sun. I did not care what they thought. All I dreamed of was finishing my life here and ending the bullying, not being accepted, not being loved and everything else which I could think of. I had planned this with precision. I had a decent hosepipe rag to stuff it with, and I knew I had done a good job. Getting my thoughts together, I shouted at them, still very angry. "Which one of you took the hosepipe out of the exhaust"? My face felt flushed, my fist held up, ready to bash the living daylights out of whoever was responsible.

All five Angels stared at me. One of them put her arms around me in an attempt to calm me down. Slowly, I began to feel less annoyed. I realised the Angel was talking to me. I stared at her. She had mousey brown hair which went halfway down her back. A pointed nose and a warm complexion. Hazel's eyes, which seemed so large I could melt in them." You see Stephen," she was in mid-sentence. "You are not ready to come up to Heaven. There are a lot of things you need to do on this earth plane before you finally leave here. We all took the hosepipe out of the car. Do not beat yourself up. Josie came to us and asked us to help save you."

I was confused. I drove home. Any thoughts of repeating this never entered my mind again.

The Angels had saved me for reasons which I found out many years later.

Two weeks later, I took an overdose, and once again, the Angels came to me and stopped me from ending my life.

Thinking about this years later, I wondered why I did not think to continue and replace the hosepipe.

The new Angels often came to me. I did not think about asking their names. I suppose I was still upset with them interfering and stopping me from ending my wretched life.

Josie was still around. I did feel guilty for seemingly letting her down.

"I have told you many times you are a very special Angel," Josie said in a gentle, soft voice. "I see you struggling, being made fun of not just with friends but in your job too. I know how hard it is. You feel lonely and unloved; you cry every night to sleep and dream of not waking up in the morning." She wrapped her arms around me as I began to cry. "Try not to cry, Stephen. One day in the future you will be famous. You are very unique, and we Angels together are going to give you gifts which no one else has."

I looked up at Josie, tears falling down my cheeks. Gently, she wiped my tears away.

"I have been so unhappy," I told her between sobs. "Why me? Why can I not be normal like any other?" I found myself holding her tightly to me. "Every day, I get made fun of. Nobody takes me seriously. I cannot do things which other guys can." I began to list things I found difficult. Making a rabbit run, fixing a cupboard, and so the list went on. Josie sat there listening to me patiently as

I went on a rant. "I wish I was able to do things like any other husband." I finished lamely.

Josie smiled. "You may not be able to do all those things, but it doesn't matter. You are a very special Angel." That word again. "The journey you are going through was your choice, Stephen. You chose this life. Maybe you have no idea why at this time, but in the future, you will get the answer." Standing up, she suddenly waved her hand. "Here is another Angel who is going to help you."

Next to Josie appeared the very Angel who spoke to me by my car. I saw her in her splendour. She was taller than Josie. Not much, but they seemed taller than me. Her long, mousy brown hair seemed to flow in an invisible breeze. "My name is Sophia." (so fire) was how she pronounced her name. She had a very soft voice. Her dress, a bright yellow, shimmered. She glided towards me. Or so it seemed.

"Stephen, you are never going to do silly things like trying to end your life again!" Sophia said in a firm but also gentle voice. "Josie has asked me to assist her from now on. We are going on a journey together."

"Does this mean Josie won't be around me much more?" I began to worry I would not see Josie anymore.

Both Angels laughed. "Of course, Josie will be with you. I will be with you too." Sophia took my left hand in hers. Her hands seemed tiny. "I am going to work alongside Josie and assist her in helping you on your journey."

I did not know what to say. I thought about what they had told me. "I have a question if you two do not mind answering?"

Josie and Sophia smiled. "What is it you wish to know?"

"You called me an Angel," I was confused. "If you are Angels, why do you say I am one? I do not look like you; I cannot appear and disappear like you can."

Josie sniggered. "Stephen, you are an EARTH ANGEL. An earth Angel is an Angel like us who wishes to come here and live as a human being. Experience the feelings humans have. Many times, you have been here, living on this planet. You are an Angel who loves being here. This is why we are around you. I have been with you since you were born," Josie reminded me. "You see things which other children and grownups cannot, "Josie waved her hand in the air. "Look at those clouds. You see shapes in them. Remember when you saw your 'wife's name in the clouds? Those dreams you had. These are gifts which you have to assist you in this earthly life."

Little did I realise at that time how much my life was going to change.

I began to realise the visions I saw many years ago were about to materialise, leading my life to places I only dreamed of going to.

Chapter 14

Spirit Land

It was New Year's Eve. Linda and I had decided to throw a party.

Years ago, just after we were married, we had a New Year's party and invited all the neighbours. We had a disco placed in a space under the stairs, plenty of food, drink and a homemade non-alcoholic punch. The noise was deafening, and the music played too well after midnight. The punch went down very well. It was only after the party finished at a silly hour in the early morning we discovered it had more punch in it than expected. It had more alcohol in it than the bottles of wine and beer. It sizzled down the sink when we finally cleared all the mess the next day. Some of the neighbours came in to help, feeling they had to help clear up as they wished to thank us for the "best party ever".

As Nicky and Dave arrived, Nicky gave me a hug. "Happy New Year from your favourite neighbour, Nicky." Dave smiled as he entered with an armful of drink and food. Linda stood there smiling.

"You may be my favourite Nicky, but I am going to meet a Nicky who is more special to me." I blurted out. I had no idea why I said this. Linda gave me a glare. Taking the food, she marched into the kitchen. Nicky smiled and followed Linda. I felt awkward. However, it was soon forgotten, and we had a wonderful time.

Nothing more was said.

I began to have a recurring dream. It was a strange dream.

A lady about my age was walking down a corridor. Following her, I knew she was important, and I had to speak to her. I never saw her face. I noticed she had blonde hair, cut short, almost like a boy's haircut. No matter how fast I rushed to catch up with her, she always seemed to be at the same distance from me.

I began to have this recurring dream shortly after the new year. It was always the same.

The company I was working for made changes to the areas we sales reps were working in. I was given South Wales and lost Sussex and Surrey.

It had been a whole ten years since I had worked in south Wales for the company, if only for a year at that time. One of the towns I had to go to was Lydney in the Forest of Dean. As I approached the market town, a feeling of dread overwhelmed me. I remember ten years ago, when I last came to Lydney, I had the same feeling of dread. Like something bad had happened. I decided to ask Josie if she had an idea why I had this horrid sensation.

"Stop for a minute," Josie instructed me. I stopped in a lay-by. I noticed Sophia was in the car, sitting in the back seat. "Relax, and we shall show you a vision."

I relaxed, and suddenly, I saw myself standing by a wooden boat. It was huge! Then I realised I was not standing but lying down beside it. I saw a man walking away from me. He had black trousers on and a baggy white shirt. I was lying on a shingle beach. I sensed there were other boats here, too.

"You saw the boat?" Sophia brought me back to the present. "You were hit on the head and killed by that man you saw walking away." Josie took hold of my hand, which I noticed now shaking. "This happened in 1876 at the Lydney docks. This man burnt your house down, and your wife died, and three children you shared with her."

I sat there stunned. "This is why I feel dread when coming here." I began to laugh out of relief.

Afterwards, I could visit Lydney without the feeling of dread.

Many years later, I went to Lydney Docks.

They were rebuilt in 1877.

One evening, Dave and Nicky invited us to their house. They had recently moved around the corner, so to speak. A ten-minute walk.

As we sat in the lounge sipping tea and eating cakes, I noticed a young girl around the age of eight appear through the wall next to where Nicky was sitting in her armchair. With her was an elderly lady who had her arm around the young girl's shoulders. I noticed the young girl had mousey brown hair, and it reminded me of Nicky's younger daughter. The older lady was of a similar build to Nicky's mother, whom we had met several times.

The girl held an enormous bouquet of flowers. The colours were vibrant, unlike the flowers I had ever seen. I asked her who the flowers were for.

The young girl pointed to Nicky. "These are for my mum." She stood there next to Nicky. "Will you tell her I love her, and she does not need to cry over me any more?".

I told her I would. "Who is the lady with you?"

The young girl smiled. "This is my great-grandmother, Nicky's mother's mum."

Meanwhile, in the room, the chat was going on. Sitting next to Linda, I gave her a little nudge.

Linda looked at me seeing a concerned look. "What is it, Steve? Have you seen a ghost?" Linda laughed.

I was not sure what to say. "Believe me or not, I have seen a ghost. Right there!" I pointed to where Nicky was sitting and showed Linda where the little girl and the grandmother stood.

"Can I ask you something? I asked Nicky tentatively. I was feeling nervous. Not sure how she would react.

Both Dave and Nicky seemed to sit up in their armchairs. Nicky began to snigger nervously. If she was nervous, then I wondered how I felt. Probably petrified. For some reason, I felt I was treading on icy ground. But looking at the girl and the woman, I took a deep breath and decided to ask.

"Can you take a girl who is around 8 years of age in spirit?" I asked. Without waiting for an answer, I continued. "A young girl is standing next to you, holding a huge bouquet of flowers, and she tells me they are for you. She is telling me you are her mum." I spurted this out before I could change my mind. "She is with your great-grandmother." I finished, sighing heavily.

I felt an electric charge fill the room. I had an awful feeling I had made a mistake.

Looking at the young girl and the lady, I noticed a look of disappointment on the young girl's face.

Both Dave and Nicky sat there stunned.

"Perhaps we should leave." I stood up. Linda slowly rose from her seat, too.

By then, the young girl and lady had decided to leave, too. I watched them as they walked through the wall, disappearing in a flash.

On the way home, I had the feeling that whatever happened that night would not end there.

"Hello Frederike," I rang our other friends as soon as we arrived home. "I had a strange experience round Nicky and Dave's this evening." I went on to explain what had happened. Frederike listened as I related the events. "I guess Nicky must have lost a child."

Frederike explained to me how she and Nicky were in the maternity hospital at the same time. "Nicky had a baby which was stillborn about 8 years ago."

"Sarah!" we both said.

"Oh, my goodness." I heard Frederike say down the phone. "That is so amazing you got her name. Nicky does not wish to talk about this. I will be very careful when you see her next time. Try not to mention anything." she warned me. "You can share it with me if you like."

The next time we all met was in the summer at Frederike and Dave's house. There was a BBQ as it was a very warm sunny day. The children ran around the garden, screaming with joy as they chased themselves, playing "catch me if you can". Sarah appeared, sitting on the grass in front of me. She gave me a hairbrush and asked me to brush her long, mousey blonde hair. I was sitting on one of the chairs. I took the brush and began to brush Sarah's hair. After a short while, Sarah stood up, smiled at me, then joined the other girls and danced around the garden. Frederike approached me.

"I saw you brushing Sarah's hair." She offered me a slice of her banoffee pie, which she knew I had a passion for. "Just be careful no one else notices," nodding her head towards Nicky. "I do not think she knows anyway, but if she says anything, do not mention Sarah by name."

For the whole of that summer, Sarah appeared often, even when I was working. Sometimes, when a photo was being taken of the girls, Sarah would join her sisters and stand between them. I could see her smiling with glee. One time, she appeared with a warm smile and a tear in her eye.

"Steve, I need to go back to Spirit land. My class starts in September. Would you like to come up there with me so I can show you my classroom?"

I stared at her. I was lost for words. "Do you actually have classrooms in Spirit land?"

Sarah laughed. "Of course we do. I would love to show you. It is such a lovely place."

To say I was surprised was an understatement. I go to Spirit Land? Luckily, I was sitting down when Sarah asked me, or I feel I would have fallen down! I gave it some thought. I did not think about it for long, just a few seconds, to be honest.

"Yes, I would love to go with you to see your classroom."

Sarah clapped her hands and gave me a kiss on the cheek. "I am so excited!" Sarah jumped up and down. I remember she was only eight years of age.

So, it was decided Sarah would take me with her after the summer holidays. I looked forward to it.

When the time came, Sarah appeared in my bedroom. "Are you ready to come along?" She grabbed my hand, and suddenly we were off. I felt myself moving up and up, feeling light. Looking around me, I saw lots of Angels with us. I was in a classroom. I noticed it had old-fashioned desks, where the student lifted the top to put the books in. There was a blackboard, too. Outside the classroom was a field of green, and I noticed a meadow. "This is my desk. "I was brought back to the classroom. Sarah was standing by a desk which was next to the window. "Look inside." She encouraged me to lift the top. I did, and inside, I saw her books and pencils.

I have no idea how long we spent there. Time seemed to stand still. It may have been minutes or hours; all I know is that time was not like it was down here.

Sarah seemed quite thoughtful.

"Steve, I can call you that, can I? I need to finish my studies here for the next 10 years, so you won't see me until I finish. I am glad I found you. I wish you were my dad."

I did not know how to answer this. 'Her dad?' I was stunned.

Sarah took my hand gently in her small one. "Come now, time to go back."

I have no idea how we arrived back, but it seemed like, in a flash, I was in my room again.

Sarah kissed me on my right cheek. "Steve, I shall come back to you in 10 years from now. I love you."

Then she was gone!

I never forgot Sarah.

That experience was not the last time I went up to Spirit Land.

Sarah was always in my thoughts.

Ten years later, she came back to me as an Angel.

Chapter 15

The Angelic Realm

Two years after my divorce, I moved away from Exmouth and bought a flat in Gloucestershire.

I remember seeing myself in a flat on my own many years ago when Josie showed me visions. The flat was bright, and on a sunny day, the room was filled all day with warm sunshine. During this time, I met Nicky. She was an assistant in a store based in Haverfordwest. She was only 5'3" tall, with short, mousey blonde hair and blue eyes. Very petite. When I saw her, I recognised she was the woman in my dreams. I later found the corridors; I followed her to a school her little boy was attending.

We got engaged!

One day, whilst out shopping, Josie approached me. "Stephen, I know you love Nicky, but I need to tell you something important".

I stared at Josie. "What is so important, you feel you need to tell me? Will I like what you say to me?"

Josie skipped as she walked alongside me. "You have found love which you never thought you would ever find in Nicky. However, when her youngest is 12, in that year, she will end your relationship. I am afraid you two will never marry."

I stopped walking, putting my shopping down on the ground, and I faced Josie. I was quite angry with her.

"Why are you telling me this now? You know how happy I am." I felt my blood boil.

Josie took a step back. I am sure she never thought I would be so hurt by the words she spoke.

"I shall come back to see you in a short while; I need to think about all this. I know it may be a shock, Stephen. You know everything I have told or shown you has been to your advantage. I have been with you all your life. Please do not be cross with me." She waved goodbye and disappeared.

Arriving in my flat, I put the shopping away. I felt really unhappy. I phoned Nicky later, and we had a wonderful conversation. "Come over, she invited me in her sweet, soft way.

I went over to see her, a two-hour journey. We shared a meal together and had a very nice weekend, as it turned out. I did not mention what Josie had told me. Somehow, deep down, I felt Josie was right. We would not marry. A close friend of mine, who worked in the hotel in Southampton, where I regularly stayed, told me, "I can see a single swan above your head. You will never marry again."

I thought about Nicky's family and how it seemed I was not accepted.

One evening, while in bed, I found myself "dreaming". It's probably astral travelling.

I saw an Angel. Taking my hand, we flew up to meet thousands of other Angels. Wrapping their wings around me, I flew higher and higher, finally reaching Spirit Land. I was shown shops, buildings and newer ones. All the time, I felt them talking to me. 'We learn as much from you as you do us. There was no sense of time. I felt warm, welcomed and at home. Then I was slowly brought back down, down, down to my bedroom.

I woke up from this 'dream', and somehow, I knew I would go up there again.

Living in South Gloucestershire, I was invited to a psychic fair in Witney, which was about an hour's journey from where I lived. Packing my aura pastels and clothes for the table, I set off feeling nervous and excited. This was the first ever event I had been invited to. The event was in a hall which was buzzing with other psychics setting up their tables, whether it was for readings or selling crystals and other goodies.

It was a very tiring day. I drew lots of auras despite another couple doing photos of auras. By 12 midday, I was falling asleep. "You need to ask them upstairs to give you the energy to work rather than your own". A lady approached me. "Try it next time before you begin working."

I did that and found I could work much more easily without getting weary. I was beginning to become a regular at the event. The organiser asked me back on several times.

I loved drawing guides and auras.

On one occasion, I was talking to a lady who was doing I.E.T. Integrated Energy Therapy. This is similar to Reiki but on a slightly higher level.

We were having a chat when another lady approached us. "This is Rosalind. She is a friend". The lady explained.

Rosalind was holding a little card. "I just had my aura photo done." Rosalind grinned happily. Holding up so we could see it,

"There should be red here in the top right-hand corner cos I sense you are not a happy bunny when you get up in the mornings."

Rosalind stared at me. "Yes, I am. I love mornings."

"No, you are not!" the other lady replied. Rosalind laughed. I pointed out a few other colours which were not in the photo, explaining what I saw.

Rosalind took a long look at me. "What do you do?" She asked me.

"I draw auras and use a crystal ball," I replied. "my table is down there; you can see my crystal ball on it." Rosalind looked in the direction I was pointing. I had won her over as she decided to have her aura drawn in colour by me. Rosalind became very good friends with me and often met up outside events.

In the meantime, the Angels would appear and take me to the Angelic Realm, as they called it. Every time was different. Shops had changed, and so had buildings. The colours of the flowers were so much more vibrant there than on Earth. "You are going to jump off this cliff." They told me on a visit up there. I stood on the edge of a cliff. All I could see was a black, purple void. Below the cliff were stars. There was nothing to land on. It's just an empty space. I was frightened to jump. I looked around me to see the Angels, too many to count, standing very close to me. "If you do not jump, we shall have to push you off the cliff."

Giving me no choice, I jumped.

Falling down into emptiness, I was not afraid to die. Except I fell all but two feet. I was standing in space! I was trying to get my head around this. Looking up at the cliff, I saw the Angels leaning over and laughing. Helping me back to their level, they surrounded me, laughing still. I did not think it was funny at all. "You have taken the Leap of Faith." They cried. I had no idea what they meant. "You know now, we are always with you, no matter what. Taking this leap of Faith shows you have nothing to fear anymore."

I did not know whether to laugh or cry. "I do not ever wish to leave here. I want to stay."

"You are not allowed to stay, Stephen. You must go back to Earth and fulfil your destiny. This is the last time we shall bring you up here. Now that you have finally taken the Leap of Faith, your destiny has now been reset."

The Angels once again brought me down to Earth, and true to their word, they never took me back again.

Oh, joy, oh joy.

One very hot day, I saw another Angel appear. She looked familiar. Long mousey brown hair, hazel eyes, slim build, about 5'5" tall. She wore a lovely dress, shimmering creamy white in the sunlight.

Sarah, the girl I met all those years ago, in fact, 10 years had flown by, had come back to me as promised. She appeared in my flat as I was doing a reading. Like 'Here I am, told you I would come and see you once I finished my studies' look on her happy face. I noticed a few freckles on her cheeks.

Sarah told me she missed her parents. Although she was stillborn, she wanted to be around them and her sisters. "My mum does not want to know me." Sarah cried. "I tried to see if they can 'see me', but they just ignore everyone who says there is a baby in spirit. I am no longer a baby. I am 18 years old, and to be totally honest, I look on you as being closer to me than my dad."

Sarah was often around my flat. Friends who pooped in sensed Sarah being around but could not see her. Sarah and I both laughed when people asked me if anyone else was in the flat. One day, my brother Kevin came to stay for a day or two.

"Who is the girl with mousey brown hair and looks about 18 years old?" He asked me when he woke up one morning. "She is standing in the doorway to your kitchen."

"Oh, you can see her then?" Without waiting for an answer, I went on, "That is Sarah." I went on to explain how we met all those years ago.

"She is very pretty," Kevin added.

As mentioned before, I was a regular reader at a psychic fair in Witney. There was another one due, so when the time came, I packed my pastels and drove to the event. As usual, it was busy. A lady approached me and asked me to draw her aura. I recognised the lady from the last visit six months ago. "Did I draw your aura last time?" I asked her.

"Yes, you did, and I loved it. I would like another aura drawn if you do not mind."

I began to draw her aura. We both got into a conversation. When I finished it, I showed her the picture.

"Wow!" she exclaimed, then reaching into her bag, which I had not taken any notice of, she drew out a folder. Opening it, there was the aura drawing I had done for her six months ago. Placing it against the one I had now just drawn for her, we noticed the drawings were virtually the same. The lady grinned. "This picture today is no different from the last one you drew." I stared at it. Apart from the very minute difference, anyone looking at it from a distance would not notice anything different at all!

"You have not done anything, which I pointed out to you last time we met." I was laughing along with her.

"No, I have not." She was now comparing the two very similar auras. "I think I should do what you suggested, then my aura will change." I agreed with her.

While at the fair, the exhibitor advertised some workshops, which I became interested in. They would be at her house. I 'signed up' for some of them.

There was a lady who had wands made out of wood exhibiting at the fair. I stopped to have a look, being drawn to them. "How much are they?" I asked. She was about my height, shoulder-length salt and pepper-coloured hair and wore spectacles.

"£15 for that one." she pointed to the one my hand was hovering over. Then, changing the subject, "You have a lot of animals following you." I stared at her. "You have an infinity with animals," She continued, "My name is Ingrid, and I am an animal communicator, which means I talk to animals. Would you like to come to my house, and I teach you how to talk to animals?"

I was stunned. I asked myself how this lady, a complete stranger, could know about all the animals which seemed to come to me when I was out and about. Cats and dogs would venture to me, and their owners would say, "My pet has never gone to a stranger."

I bought a wand which she helped me to choose. Then I agreed to go to her house and do a one-day course on Animal communication.

One day, I went to Witney to the house where I was taking part in a workshop. I was told to park in a particular car park, about half a mile from the house. "Take the path through the park and follow it, turn this way and that, the house is on your left". I began to walk, but in a short while, I was completely lost. I was told to look up into the sky. There in the sky, gently floating down, was a white feather. It danced in front of me and began to move, telling me to follow. I realised this was an Angel coming to help me. The feather danced and stopped often to see whether I was following. Turning down one path, then another, always waiting for me to catch up. I knew it was not Josie.

The Angel was always at my waist height. Dancing merrily in front of me. Then, a sharp left, and there was the house I was looking for. I thanked her. She came closer to me and touched my nose. Then, watching her, she went up and up into the sky and disappeared.

I went into the house.

There were all sorts of one-day workshops to choose from. There were meditation workshops tarot, and certain readers who did not attend the fairs came here to do readings as well. I booked up to have a reading from a well-known reader. I remember her name was Sharon. She told me she could see me moving house, drawing and painting (I had been told that in many readings) and using different tools to read. I was just drawing auras at this time.

Chapter 16.

Daisy.

I often used to like watching Animal Magic as a child. Johnny Morris was the presenter who 'talked' to the animals in the zoo. I always had a strange connection with animals, which I never understood. I had a little blue and white budgie when I was 6 years old. I say he was mine as although it was a family 'pet', he would always sit on my finger when I put my hand in the cage. He would chirp and get excited whenever I approached him. I noticed he did not do this whenever his brother and sisters wanted to 'play' with him. If we let him out of his cage, he would fly around the lounge and then come and sit briefly on my shoulder.

I became aware that other pets would come up to me and, with tails wagging, lick my face and run around me. It never happened to the other children who lived on our estate.

When I lived in Exmouth with our pets, we had a cat which we named Polly. I remember one morning, as I was just about to go out of the house to work, Polly meowed at me. I had a feeling she was saying 'goodbye'. As I left home for the day, I muttered to my youngest daughter, who was holding her, "Try to keep Polly in today". I knew that would never happen as Polly loved to go outside.

When I came home later that evening, my next-door neighbour grabbed me. "Come here; I have some very bad news for you." I followed him into his garden shed, where he lifted up a cloth, which I noticed was on the bench. Under it was Polly. "I found her by the side of the road, by the steps." I wiped away the tears in my eyes. "I did not take it round to your house, as I felt it better if you did."

Picking Polly up, I took her home. The thought of what I had from Polly that morning was haunting me. Later, when we had all calmed down, I told the family what Polly had told me that morning. "I do not know how she knew she was going to die, but I am certain the way she meowed at me this morning was telling me she was going. You remember when I said, try to keep her in"? I finished, tears filling my eyes again. I had no idea how I knew Polly was able to 'connect 'with me.

These thoughts were with me as I drove to Swindon to take part in the one-day Animal Communication workshop. I was both very excited and nervous.

Ingrid met me at her front door, "Come in and make yourself comfortable. You will be working with my pet dog; her name is Daisy."

I walked into the lounge and sat down on a chair by a table. Offering me a cup of coffee, we had a talk about the day. "You will be walking out of here knowing you can talk to animals. You will get a certificate and a book to help you in this course". Ingrid picked a book from a shelf on a bookcase and placed it in front of me. "Do not open the book yet". Ingrid instructed me as my hand ventured towards the book. Explaining further about the course, I began to wonder if I could do it. Ingrid must have seen the concerned look on my face. "I have been teaching this for many years, and I must point out, NOBODY has failed". Then, as an afterthought, "You are okay with large dogs"? Ingrid then rose from her seat and fetched Daisy in.

Daisy was indeed quite a large dog and one breed I was afraid of. A Rottweiler.

Seeing my fear, Ingrid told me not to worry. "She is a gentle animal and will not bite you."

The morning went on, and as I began to relax, I stepped into the role of talking to Daisy. "She is showing me a wooden gate on a path leading down to the sea." I began. "The beach has shingles rather than sand, and Daisy is excited to be there."

Ingrid smiled. "Well done. Can you pick anything else up?" She encouraged me.

I concentrated on Daisy as instructed. "This was a daily walk she took in the morning before breakfast on a holiday. I feel you stayed in a caravan."

Ingrid smiled and clapped her hands. "That is very good. We went on a holiday last year, and she did go for a walk to the beach with my husband. We stayed in a caravan, too,"

My confidence grew, and I became more bold as the day wore on.

Finally, the course was coming to an end. "You are an amazing student," Ingrid told me. "Before we finish the course, I would like you to talk to Daisy and see what she has to tell you."

Once again, I took a deep breath, connected with Daisy and asked her permission to talk to her.

Suddenly, I was getting lots of pictures. "She was in Battersea dog's home. Her previous owners used to stub cigarettes out her back and thighs. Tied her to a chain in a very small yard." I was seeing all this, and then I had something else. "You know she does not act in a way dogs usually do? I am getting the answer to why she is not 'normal." I stopped. "It is so ridiculous. I feel if I said it, you would think I am mad!"

Ingrid stared at me. With a stern voice, she spoke. "How many times have you been told what you get from spirit may not sound right to you but makes sense to the person who hears it?" Ingrid gave me a wag of her finger. "Now tell me what Daisy told you."

I took a very deep breath. "Daisy tells me why she is not like any other dog," I took another breath. Ingrid smiled warmly, wanting me to finish. "You had a baby who died at 15 months. The soul of that little boy is within Daisy. This is why she is not like any other dog you have had in the past."

I finished and sat back in my seat, not forgetting to 'thank Daisy' for her help.

Ingrid's reaction to this revelation was astounding. Standing up, she paced around the room. "Amazing, you are only the second student, and I have taught thousands to talk to animals, who picked that up. Yes, my baby boy's soul is in Daisy." Passing me my certificate, she hugged me.

"I am feeling jealous of giving you this certificate. You will be a fine teacher. One of the best students I have taught." We went on to chat for a little longer before I left.

I still met up with Ingrid at Psychic Fairs, and we laughed and joked about that wonderful day we both had. I know that particular course was a life-changing one for me. I went on to teach many students how to 'talk' to animals and pets.

Over the years since, I have learned how to 'connect' with pets via photographs. I love being able to talk to animals. Whether it is a cat, dog, horse, rabbit or even a guinea pig, bringing smiles to people's faces is rewarding.

Shortly following my course, I visited Marianne and Roger in Exmouth. They had a golden retriever named Ben. "I wonder if you can talk to Ben?" Marianne asked me one day. "Let's see what he tells you".

We were both in the kitchen, and Ben was making his usual fuss of me, trying to jump onto my lap as I sat on a chair. "Down, Ben." Marianne put her hand on Ben's head and pushed him gently down so he was now sitting next to me. I noticed he had a sad look on his face, knowing how much she loved making a fuss when I arrived. "We will be in the other room." The other room was the lounge.

I focussed on Ben, who was quite content to lie down on her blanket. "Hello, Ben. Is it alright for me to speak with you?" I asked him, just as I was taught. I waited, and after a few seconds, I saw, much to my joy, a response. Ben lifted his head, and his eyes focussed on me. Ben told me all about the holiday they had in Holland. I was surprised at how easy it was to connect and have a conversation with him. After we finished, I went into the lounge, where Marianne and Roger were having a quiet conversation and watching their favourite program, the X-Files. Dana was named after one of the main characters in the show.

"Did he speak to you?" Marianne asked excitedly. Before I could answer, "What did he tell you? Does he love living with us? Is he lonely when we go out to work, despite us leaving the radio in for him to listen to?" All these questions.

I took a deep breath and began to tell them what Ben had told me. "You went to a Zoo in Holland, and though we do not allow dogs, except guide dogs, in the Zoos in the U.K.U.K., in Holland, you are allowed to bring them in. Ben told me about the sea lions and how he loved watching them jump up and down in the water. He wanted to watch them all day. There was a gorilla, Ben barked at. He doesn't mind you going to work, as he tells me; he looks forward to you taking him out for a walk once you arrive home." I went on to say lots of other things which Ben had shown me.

Marianne and Roger sat there open-mouthed in shock. "You are so right. Ben did love the sea lions and barked at the gorilla. That is so amazing, you talked to him."

I often visited Marianne and Roger when I lived in Exmouth.

Ben loved me as we built up an unusual connection. He would tell me how he felt when Roger and Marianne went to work. Every time I sat down on their sofa, he would run in and jump on top of me. Being a large breed, I was knocked sideways as he smothered me with licks and made a fuss of me.

Chapter 17

Agnetha and Henry

I practically lived in Marianne's house, as they often invited me around. They had a large kitchen at the back, which led into the lounge. Upstairs were three bedrooms, one of which was a box room where Roger had his 'office'. There was a window facing the landing at the top of the stairs. To the left was the bathroom and a separate toilet.

Every time I went up the stairs, I saw a lady standing on the landing. I often greeted her as she stood serenely beside a dressing table which was in front of the window. I often joked she was not allowed to follow me into the toilet. I used to tell Marianne there was this woman at the top of the stairs, standing on the landing. "Between Roger's office and the second bedroom ". I explained. "She does not say anything, just stands there". I went on. "Have you seen or sensed there is someone there"? I asked Marianne.

Marianne had not. We went up the stairs, and I pointed to where the lady was. "There she is!" I said. Marianne looked to where my finger was pointing. She could not see her. "Sorry, Steve, I cannot see or feel anything."

I stared at Marianne. "Honestly, she is standing right in front of that dressing table." I could not understand why Marianne, who had seen spirit and auras when we went to workshops, could not see this woman.

The lady was about 5' 6" and had wavy, rather short hair, reddish brown, or, as we would say, a brunette. She had large brown eyes and wore a lovely colourful dress which fell down to just below her knees. I noticed she wore black-laced shoes. No high heels, I noticed.

I nodded to the woman on the stairs. She smiled and then seemed to disappear like a puff of smoke.

"Why is she in my house?" Marianne asked as we stood in the kitchen. Marianne had put the kettle on for us. Roger was in the lounge, falling asleep.

"I have no idea why she is here. I never thought about asking her." I took the cup of coffee Marianne offered me and followed her into the lounge. There was a large television in the corner, still on, but hardly any sound. Roger was dozing in an armchair. We both sat on a sofa and talked about this woman up the stairs. Marianne was always keen to find out more about Spirituality and loved talking about the things we had learned.

"How long do you think she has been upstairs? Why does she not come down here and see us?" The questions flowed from Marianne, and I had a job to answer before another question was asked.

All I knew from my experience was that this woman had been in this house ever since I first visited. I did not take too much notice as I thought both Marianne and Roger had known this 'Spirit' was there. I had been friends with Marianne and Roger for some years now, and seeing this woman there was normal.

"Next time I see her, I shall ask her what she is doing in your house if you like," I responded to Marianne's many questions. "I am not that good. I can get the full facts, but I shall try."

Marianne laughed with excitement. I loved the innocent way she took this in. "Oh yes, please do. I am worried she may be lost or something." When Marianne got excited, her Dutch accent was much more pronounced.

Marianne and Roger had two golden retrievers, Ben and Sammy, previously before Dana. They were lovely animals and always made a fuss of me when I visited them. Ben, especially, would stick his nose anywhere he could reach me, even knocking me over at times. They were quite old when I first met them. And after a few years, sadly, they went to 'pet heaven.'

We would often 'see' them running around the house playfully. It was nice to know that even though they had left us, they were still in the house. Mostly downstairs, I noticed.

"They were not allowed upstairs," Marianne explained. "Probably why we only see them downstairs."

Shortly after this sad episode, they decided to buy another Golden Retriever from a breeder in Newton Abbot. "Would you like to come with us to help us choose one?" they asked me.

I was shocked, to say the least. Me, help them choose another pet? I was so happy to be part of this family I accepted the kind offer.

The very next week, we all travelled in Marianne's car to see the dog. Roger could not drive, so Marianne drove in her car. It was a right-hand drive, which was a Dutch-registered model.

The breeder was a lovely lady. Wavy blonde hair and a gushing personality. Her husband let her do all the talking. He spent most of the time in the background or making tea.

"If you come into the sitting room, I shall bring the mother in to meet you. Be careful, though, as she is a lively animal and may well jump up and possibly knock you over."

She disappeared and left us three standing in the room. There was a large sofa on one end by the wall where I stood. A clock ticked loudly on the mantle piece.

Suddenly, the door slammed open, and in bounced the mother, who immediately made a beeline for me! Jumping up, she bowled me over. I fell onto the sofa, and then she sat on top of me, pinning me down and licking my face. I could hear a commotion going on but could not move. I heard someone muffle, "Is he the one who is buying this puppy?"

Eventually, someone pulled the animal off me. Everyone was laughing.

Managing to stand up again, I brushed myself down and saw everyone smiling.

"She really has taken to you." The breeder remarked. "I have never seen do that before."

Shortly after, once I had recovered from being smothered by a full-grown Golden Retriever, the puppy was brought in. She was so tiny compared to her mum and, like her mother, made a beeline for me. Trying to jump up, running around my feet.

"She seems to like you, "The breeder said. "Are you going to buy her?"

"No, we are," Marianne laughed. "We are naming her Dana. From the Files." She added.

As we drove home, Marianne glanced into the rearview mirror so she could see me sitting in the backseat. "Dana likes you. I think she will ask you, when you visit, to take her out for lopens." Using the Dutch word for walkies.

Roger laughed. Wiping the sweat off his head with a handkerchief, he half turned his head towards me. "I can say you and Dana will get on. I was shocked at how the mother bowled you over." He began laughing. "That was so funny. Seeing her on top of you, almost buried under her on the sofa. I wish I had a camera." He added.

It was quite comical, thinking about it after. But at the time, no way was it! Having a great lump sitting on you.

Eventually, we arrived home. The house seemed cold and empty since Ben had gone. Marianne was excited to get a new puppy. "She will love it here. I hope she likes her new bed, the garden." Marianne was so happy. Both Roger and I felt the energy. Most of the day, we discuss how Dana may fit in. "Do you think she may 'see' Ben and Sammy?"

she finally got around to asking me a direct question. I was not expecting that!

"I have no idea." I quietly replied. "Most animals can see other pets who have passed over, so perhaps you may find Dana seemingly staring into space."

Dana arrived a week later. Marianne invited me over to see Dana. When I arrived, there was a lot of noise going on in the house. A puppy barking and lots of laughter. Marianne opened the front door. There was a scampering of feet on wooden floors, which they had in their house, followed by Dana trying hard to reach me. We managed to close the door. Walking into the kitchen, with Dana trying hard to jump up to lick my face, I was met by other members of her family. Now I understood what all the noise was about.

Dana loved the attention. Despite playing with her, she never seemed to tire of wanting more.

One time, when I visited, Marianne told me she wanted to have a private word with me. Seeing a worried look on my face, she laughed. "No, it is not bad. I cannot talk to Roger, as he does not really believe in this stuff." I guessed correctly. She was referring to 'Spiritual' things. Taking me out into the garden, she explained. "We went to Plymouth and spoke to a spiritual woman. I told her there was a gentleman in our house. She told me to find the best medium I know to clear the ghost. So I am asking you if you can help us."

"Me? What do you mean by me being the best medium you know?" I asked her. I felt my jaw fall open in shock. "I am not the right one for this. We know lots of mediums." I went on to name a few. Marianne smiled. "I believe in you,

Steve. As far as I am concerned, you are the best medium I have ever known." She went on to explain her dilemma. "I have felt a presence in the spare bedroom. I have no idea what it is." By now, we were heading back into the kitchen. "This happened recently. The lady we spoke to says we should find a good medium who can help us."

I thought about this for a few minutes. Questions by the dozen filled my head. Marianne offered me a cup of coffee, which I took gratefully. She always knew what I loved.

"When exactly did you notice this spirit?"

Marianne sat down on a chair and thought. "I think a few weeks ago, I went into the spare room and felt a strong presence there. I think it may be a man". She finished suddenly. "Why has he appeared so suddenly?"

I sipped my hot coffee. Thinking about this, an idea sprang. "I wonder if this man has anything to do with the woman on the landing."

Marianne clapped her hands. "This is why I choose you rather than anyone else. You are amazing!"

I had no reply to this. It was an educated guess. The woman on the landing had been there in the house for as long as I had been friends with Marianne and Roger. Why was she there? What was she there for? Was there a connection with this man, who had suddenly 'appeared'?

We went upstairs and entered the spare room. This was adjacent to Roger's office. Immediately, I felt a strange presence in the room, which I had not noticed before. I slowly looked around, trying to see whether I could feel someone there. Although I knew there was something here, I could not see it at that time.

Marianne was very close to me. Her 6'1" height dwarfed me. "Can you feel anything?" she asked.

I felt a cold air in the room. I mentioned this. I needed to think about this. I had a strong sense this apparition was connected to the lady on the landing. How I did not know at this point.

Somehow, I had a feeling I would find out.

Not long after, we arranged for me to try and do a house clearance. I was invited round for a meal. Marianne loved cooking and made some lovely Dutch dishes. After we had eaten, a friend of hers, Rose, came round. Marianne had invited her. Rose, I had met before. She was very spiritual and often told us stories of seeing Sam and Ben running around downstairs and through the window into the garden. "Their feet are a foot off the ground." She would tell us.

"Stephen is here to help us to clear this spirit who is in the spare room," Marianne explained to Rose.

We went upstairs. There on the landing was the woman standing by the dressing table. I decided to ask her name. Why I had not thought of this before was a mystery. Marianne and Rose were standing just behind me.

"My name is Agnetha," she replied with a beam on her face. "My husband is called Henry." She added.

The three of us walked into the spare bedroom. It was quite dark in there as the curtains were drawn. I sensed an atmosphere in here. The air grew cold, and I had goosebumps on my arms. There, over the bed, was a man standing by the wall and through the bed. He was quite tall, about 5'11" and wore a hat. Dressed in a suit, he had a smile on his face. I asked him who he was.

"Oh, you can see me then," (Why do they always ask that?) "My name is Henry, and Agnes is my lovely wife. She has been here waiting for me to come and take her to Heaven." He finished.

I looked out into the landing and saw Agnes standing there. "I thought she told me her name was Agnetha," I told Henry.

Henry went on to explain.

His parents owned a mansion not too far from Exmouth. Agnes was a servant girl who worked downstairs' scrubbing floors on her hands and knees. He had taken a liking to Agnes." I noticed how pretty she was, and I fell in love with her." Unfortunately, his parents told him he was not allowed to mix with the servants as they were not good enough for his stature. He arranged to meet up with Agnes secretly. Agnes was quite shy. They both knew the danger of being found out. She would lose her job, and Henry could well find himself being punished.

Eventually, they decided to get married. If Agnes lost her job, Henry promised to look after her. Henry's parents disowned him and took away his inheritance, leaving him virtually penniless. His love for Agnes was enough for them to leave and be together.

Agnes changed her name to Agnetha, as it sounded posh, Henry went on to explain. They moved to Exmouth and lived in a house just two blocks from where Marianne and Roger lived.

Henry told me he died in 1965.

I told both Agnetha and Henry they would be together again. Henry was worried as his family were still angry, and this is why Agnetha was stuck here. She was frightened to face the wrath of his family.

Marianne, Rose and I sat down on the bed. I quickly explained fully what we were going to do to Henry. Agnetha stepped into the room.

As we began, a strong wind suddenly blew around the room. It was like a mini tornado, very cold, but we knew this would not prevent us from doing the work.

"Visualise a silver escalator and a bright light at the bottom and top of it!" I found myself shouting as the noise was deafening. The wind whipped around the bedroom. I saw Henry travelling up the escalator and standing at the very top. He looked back down on us. "Agnetha, try and step on the escalator." I encouraged her. She slowly stepped on it, almost hesitating.

"Thank you, Steve. Thank you for helping me. I waited in this house for you. I have no idea how long it has been, but I am glad you arrived to help us." With that, she went up the escalator to the bright light, where Henry stood. Turning around, she waved goodbye, mouthing the words 'Thank you." I thought I saw a tear in her eyes. I began to cry.

The wind in the room began to abate to a breeze, which eventually died out. Both Rose and Marianne were exhausted. It was then we remembered Roger was in the other small room, next door, which he called his 'office'. Roger was in a bad way. The wind and energy which drove it had entered the office, with Roger feeling the full force of it all. Poor Roger had his head on his desk. He had no idea what we had done.

It took us a long time to understand what really had taken place.

We never saw Agnetha or Henry again.

Chapter 18

Road trip with Angels.

One day, I woke up with a start. I knew there was someone with me, but I had no idea who it was. Getting out of bed and wiping the sleepy dust from my eyes, I strolled into the living room of my flat. The windows were on a latch. I could close the windows and leave enough space for air to come in. I noticed, in the middle of the floor, a brown feather. There was no way that feather had come in the windows. I bent down to pick it up, and suddenly Josie appeared.

"Daniel has been here!" Josie exclaimed excitedly. And then she danced round the room.

I had no idea why he should leave a feather in my flat. I turned to Josie, who now decided to sit on my sofa, crossing her legs. Placing her hands on her lap, she gave me a winning smile. "Daniel is an Angel who can bring you the abundance you need. He will assist you in overcoming remorse for any mistakes you may have made in the past," Josie explained. "he is quite the character once you get to know him." Josie stared up at the ceiling, pondering. "I think he may be here to help you with your speech and assist you in front of an audience. You love to interpret dreams, and Daniel was good at doing that." Josie then sat back on the sofa and relaxed.

I went into the kitchen to make myself a cup of coffee. Josie was relaxing meanwhile on the sofa. I often had a stutter and had difficulty expressing myself, so this made sense. "I hope he may be able to help me". I was quite open to allowing new Angels to come into my life. No matter who it may be, Josie was always the most important Angel.

Josie was such a lovely Angel. I could share anything with her and know she would find answers, even if she did not know everything.

Perhaps Daniel was coming in to help me with my speech. I had no idea.

On another day, not too long after, I met Daniel. He stood in my living room and just smiled. "Hello, Stephen, I am Daniel". He stood about my height, possibly a little taller. I noticed he had reddish brown hair, which was quite long. When I say long, I mean it grew past his ears and flirted with his neck. He wore a brown jacket and brown shoes. His shirt was yellow in colour, which complimented his brown jacket.

"I am here to help you with your Healing and speech, confidence, and overcoming the mistakes you feel hold you back." He said. Almost rushing it out before I could interject.

I sat there open-mouthed. "Okay…….. So where do we start?"

Over the next few months, Daniel worked with me. We often had meditations, where he led me on journeys to find my true self. I went with him willingly, finding confidence and happiness within me, which, up to then, I had never realised I had. He helped me in interpreting dreams, which I was excited about. My speech improved, although often when I was stressed, my stutter came back with a vengeance.

"I am done," Daniel told me one day. "You have now completed the tasks which I have set you. I wish you well." With that, just as abruptly as he first arrived, Daniel went. I never saw him again.

Josie was always in the distance when Daniel was around, but now she was with me all the time. In my face, you could say.

"I am so pleased," Josie said. "You are going to find new friends, and doors are now opening for you. Just wait and see. It is about time you flourished."

I listened to her with eyes wide open. I had no real idea what she meant, but Josie had always had my interests at heart and had never let me down.

I was still attending events in Marlowe and Witney. One of my friends, Yvonne, who was a Reiki master, asked me one day if I would like to join her at an event in Stanstead. "You can do your animal communication, and I can do Reiki on them."

I drove over to Marlowe, where we jumped into her car, and we made our way to Stanstead. Four Angels sat in the back seat. I saw them sitting quietly as I glanced in the mirror. I could see Josie, Sofia, Sarah and another who I had no idea.

As we approached the outskirts of Stanstead, Yvonne told me she was not too sure exactly where the event was. The Sat Nav told her to go over a roundabout.

"As you go over the roundabout," The four Angels spoke to me. "There is a red sports car parked on the left-hand side of the road, about three miles from here. 50 yards after the car is a small lane, which you need to turn up, and this will bring you to the event." I passed the message on to Yvonne.

"Wow! You do have a strong connection with your Angels." She replied as we journeyed down the road. A few minutes later, we saw a red sports car parked on the left-hand side, just as the Angels had told us. "There is the red car. The turning is just a few yards after where it is parked!"

The event was quite a busy affair. The weather was hot and sunny. We both sheltered under a marque. I had my animal tarot cards with me, which I used occasionally. We both enjoyed the hours spent, Yvonne practising Reiki on the pets, mostly dogs. There were a few other pets which customers brought along. One had a rabbit, which I thought was quite strange. I connected with the pets, either by 'talking to them' or offering photo readings. I loved reading the photos, which is a form of psychometry.

When the event had finished, the organiser invited us both into her house for a meal. It turned out to be tea and lots of chocolate biscuits. The house had lino on all the floors rather than carpets. I noticed a strong doggy smell which pervaded the air.

"Can you tell me why this one keeps on barking and doesn't sit down for long?" pointing to a dog which was running around barking all the time. The organiser had Faith in me that I could answer everything. I heard after the clients who came to see me had told her how good they thought I was.

I relaxed and tried to focus on the dog. He looked quite scruffy if I was to be honest. Quite a large breed, not quite as big as a Labrador or even a golden retriever, I thought, thinking of Ben. I guessed he was some sort of Spaniel or Beagle cross.

"I am getting he has been a rescue dog and was not treated at all well by the last people who owned him," I began. "He does not like noise and certain tall men, especially if they have boots on."

The organiser opened her mouth, and I saw her jaw drop. Leaning forward in her chair, she was paying a lot of attention. Yvonne, on the other hand, just sat in her chair, smiling.

I went on to explain his barking. "He tells me he is protecting you. He is frightened he may be taken away from this house, and he barks to try to tell you he loves you. He also needs attention. He feels threatened by all the other dogs you have." There were about five dogs which I knew of. "If you give him a lot of fuss and try to make him feel he is more important than the others, he will stop barking and become more settled."

When we left, the dog in question came towards me, nuzzling his face against my tummy. Trying to jump up, the owner told him off. I smiled.

Many years later, I saw the owner again at an event in South Wales. She told me after I left, she tried making more fuss with him, and the dog did stop barking and running around. It was nice to get some feedback, even though it was so long after.

I now had three Angels constantly with me. Josie, Sarah and Sofia.

Sarah is only 5'6" tall and has very dark, almost black hair, which falls halfway down her back. She often wears a flowery salmon pink coloured dress. She has huge dark brown eyes. In her hands, she carries a two-edged sword. "I protect you," She reminds me often. "The sword, protect you from being attacked from behind, as I stand behind you. Then, when I stand with you, I take your hand, as Josie allows." She went on, glancing at Josie, who stood with her, nodding her head in acknowledgement. "I walk in front of you and use the other side of my sword to cut down the barriers which may appear." Then Sarah came in close and kissed me. "I shall work with you. Anyone who needs help in any way, I shall go to them. You will be given a sign from me, so you know who I wish to help. These people will need help."

Sofia is a lovely, warm Angel. I was cross with her, years ago, when she took the hosepipe out of the car, that night when I had decided to leave this Earth.

She is a little taller than me. Around 5'11". When she appears, which is not often, I may add, she comes on a vibration of peace, tranquillity, hope, confidence and 'knowing.' She wears a long creamy white dress, decorated with rustic flowers and lots of jewellery. She has a lovely, warm smile and soft green eyes. "I am here to help you in ways you do not yet understand. I am going to give you visions of the past, your past and other people's past, too."

I stood there aghast!

Josie came forward. "Now is not time to worry or ponder, Stephen. Sofia has decided she wishes to say sorry for the hurt and anger you had and still have since that time you wished to end your life. She knows there are times when you still look back and question why did she stop you." Taking my hand in her smaller one, she said, "I always knew you were special from the day you were born. You have so many gifts. You now have three 'charmed ones' to help you on your journey.

I had no idea what that journey would be.

"I am going to show you a vision of your past," Sofia told me one day.

Chapter 19

Auschwitz

I always feel blessed to be able to talk to my Angels and hear them, see them and laugh and cry with them.

I often wonder if I could not see or hear them, where I would be today.

One day, I was in my lonely flat, contemplating my life and thinking about the future and where I would end up. I often did this, even though throughout my days, Angels always led me to where I should be. I know I saw myself in a flat when I was just 9 years old.

Sofia appeared. "Hi Stephen, I thought I would come to see you as it is time you had some answers."

I sat there staring at her. "What do you mean by you giving me answers?" I sat up straighter. "What do you think I need to know?"

"May I sit down next to you?" Sofia motioned towards the two-seater sofa I was sitting on. Her creamy white and pink dress seemed to flow around her as she moved towards me. There was an invisible breeze which rose her hair and made it seem to swirl.

Without waiting for an answer, Sofia sat down by my side. She turned sideways so she could look directly into my face. "First of all," she began, smiling warmly as she placed her delicate hands on my knees, "Josie knows I am here, and she agrees with me it is time for you to know about Auschwitz. May I begin?"

I remembered all those nightmares I had growing up. The vision I saw of me on a train and entering Auschwitz all those years ago, thought about the books I read about the Jews in the concentration camps during the war, the overwhelming thought I had been there in a past life. Who was I? Where was I born? I knew now I would get the answers from Sofia. I felt excited and frightened at the same time. "Am I ready for this?" I asked myself.

I took one of Sofia's hands and held it tight. "I would love to know the truth. This may help me to understand why I am who I am now." I thought about lots of things. Having those dreams, and in a practicable way, having an eating disorder.

"Close your eyes and relax," Sofia placed her hands on my cheeks and caressed me. "I am going to lead you through a vision. Do not be frightened; watch what happens, knowing you are seeing past events which happened a long time ago."

I closed my eyes.

Sofia's voice filled my head, then silence.

I was within a crowd of people, some dressed smartly, some in rags. Children were skipping and playing in the dusty street. The next thing I was on a train. It was packed!

I managed to get to the window, but there was no glass. There were slats rather than windows. I realised this was an old train used to transport cattle. I felt claustrophobic. I tried to reach out and get some air to breathe. Nearby, I noticed a man. He was quite big in build, with balding hair which he had combed across his head. He wore a brown jacket and dark brown trousers. He carried a huge brown suitcase, which he held on to as if his life depended on it.

The carriage was crammed with people, no room to sit down. The children cried out, wanting fresh air and room to play. Then I noticed the train had stopped. Someone slid open a door and threw some apples and a few bottles of water into the cabin before the doors were closed again. We all scrambled to get the apples, and thankfully, most of us managed to get some to help quench our thirst. I had no idea how long we stayed without moving. One day, it may have been about five days later, the train suddenly gave a shunt forward, and I nearly fell over. I looked around the carriage; the man was lying on the floor. He smelt rotten. A few others were lying down. I realised they had died. A little further on, I noticed a change in the scenery as it sped by. It was flatter, with hardly any trees. The train began to slow down. As I looked out the slats, I saw people standing on a platform, waving a greeting to us. I noticed German soldiers, either with guns or holding a leash with dogs, who were barking. The train stopped abruptly, and I managed to hold on to a man who was leaning against the side to stop myself from falling over. My legs were tired and aching. I knew if I fell over, I would not get up.

The doors slid open, and outside voices shouted in German for us to get out quickly. We departed the train and landed on the platform. There were not many of us left alive in the carriage. I was pushed into a queue. Dogs barked and snarled at us. Guns were pushed into our bodies to encourage us to keep moving. Other people dressed in black, grey-striped clothes smiled, telling us not to be afraid.

There were two queues. I was on the right-hand side, nearer the train. The left queue was mainly all the old people and little children. I looked forward and saw an archway saying Welcome to Auschwitz. As I walked forward, I noticed a tall, slim chimney stack in the distance on the right as we entered the camp. White smoke was billowing out of it.

"Namen!" I was at the front facing a desk with a man asking me my name. "Josef… Josef Van De Haart," I replied. "I came from Rotterdam, and I am 16 years old," I replied to his other questions.

I was led to a building where we were told to take off all our clothing and have a shower. The guys in the stripey clothes, I realised, were Jews who were helping the Germans. All items of jewellery were to be placed on the trays provided. We were led to a room where we took all our clothing off. Men, boys and women, no time to get embarrassed. We were ushered into a large open room; I noticed what I realised were shower heads hanging down from the ceiling. The room was packed, but not as badly on the train. Then, with a shock, cold water splashed on us, accompanied by a strong odour of carbolic. After the shower, we were given our items back.

I saw tall-story buildings, which were the houses we were to live in. I noticed, as I entered the camp, single-storied buildings on the left, which were down another road. Bands played music, and children played and sang happy songs, although faces told a completely different story.

I felt Sofia as she slowly brought me back into the room. "You saw, didn't you."

"Yes, I did. I saw myself being transported into Auschwitz." I told her my vision. Although it had seemed ages, the vision had only lasted around 10 minutes.

"Stephen, you did well. I realise it may give you the answers you are looking for," Sofia clapped her hands and then stood up, facing me. She seemed so happy. "The next time I see you, not today, as this has been enough for one vision, I am going to show you what happened when you were there. How and why you died in that life."

It was strange knowing a past life and actually remembering it. The vision was not like a past life meditation (I had been on one before.) It was like 'looking back on a memory' and actually being there. Feeling the emotions which one does not get in a past life regeneration.

Thinking about Josef (Yes, I now knew my name,) I felt more comfortable with myself. I remembered Rotterdam, how it was destroyed by the Nazis, as they constantly bombed the city. I remembered my birthday. Born on April 20th 1925.

I understood why I was infatuated with the Holocaust. Reading many books about the Jews in the Second World

War. I watched many movies, but there were a lot of others I could not and still unable to watch. What happened in Auschwitz was horrific.

Over the next few weeks, I saw many more visions, which Sofia gave to me. I saw myself working in a kind of 'factory' sewing shirts, which we Jews were told to wear. The rooms we slept in were crowded. Bunk beds were set up, three beds at a time. Single beds with a grey sheet on the bed for us to lay on. The men were all put together, and the women separated. Often, it was so cold it was difficult to get to sleep. Food was scarce. Every now and then, a Red Cross lorry would appear, with food being given to us. The S.S.S.S. guards distributed the food as they saw fit, which meant not all received any bread or supplements. The bread was often hard. Water we mainly got from melting snow in the winter. During other times, although the water was available, we had to dodge the guards and their dogs to get to a tap.

One November morning, I woke up early. It was not quite dawn. I felt cold, not actually freezing cold. I shivered, although there were plenty of other 'inmates' around. I lay there wrapping the scant bedding around me, trying to get some warmth. Someone below me gave a little cough. I leaned over my bunk and looked down at the guy below me. "You awake?" I whispered.

"Yes, but it was not you who woke me up." He pointed out to me to take any thoughts I had had. "What woke you up?" he asked me.

"The cold woke me up," I replied. "I am not sure, but I feel something may happen today." I was still shaking with the cold.

"I think there may be a load of new people coming today." The man below me whispered.

True enough, a train turned up at the far end of the 'town' as it was now called by the Germans. A band was playing, and people, chosen by the commandment, sang joyful songs. I thought about the time I had arrived, hearing the music and the joyful singing. I know now it is all false to give the impression we love living here.

The snow fell, and soon, everything was covered in a thick blanket of fresh snow. At least we knew we could melt it for water, to quench our thirst.

Sofia often aided me in 'seeing' this life. I felt like I was in a movie. Seeing all this happening, knowing this was me, I felt sad but also excited to know why I am the person I am now. Some of the questions< I have asked myself were being answered now as I watched my past.

My fear of being in a closed space is the eating disorder I have had since I was twelve years old. There were other situations in this life I learned later came from that life.

Sofia showed me another vision.

I was in the middle of the town. It had been snowing. I was shivering with the cold. I saw a young girl standing nearby. She was around sixteen years old, with muddy brown hair, which, on a normal day, would have been quite wavy. I noticed she was not as thin as myself, so she must have recently arrived. She was only about 5'4". Her name was Gisella, and she was Hungarian. I involuntarily touched her on her left hand. I felt sorry for her, knowing the life we can expect here.

I was grabbed roughly by the S.S. guards, who then dragged me to a clearing in the middle of the 'Town' and bludgeoned me to death.

I came out of the vision. Sofia was holding my hand. "I saw it too," she told me. "Now you know how you died and why."

I was taken aback. "I did not know Jews were bludgeoned to death," I stuttered. "I know we were either gassed or shot, but I was bludgeoned to death for just touching that girl on her hand? I had a feeling that not many Jews were bludgeoned to death. The next time I saw Marianne, I told her what I had seen. She was aghast!

"You actually know your name?" she was shocked. "I wish I knew a past life like you can see yours." Then, sitting down on the sofa, she asked me lots of questions, "How did you manage to see this? what was it like in Auschwitz?" Then she calmed down. "How do you feel, knowing this happened in a past life?"

I sat there pondering. "I feel sad that I was there, but knowing who I was, how and why I died, makes me feel I have answers." I thought about my life and what I had learned growing up. Then, I had an awakening!

I knew then why I was born with a brain hemorrhage. It was not due to my premature birth, as I was led to believe. I realised that maybe the past life had everything to do with this one, in more ways than I had imagined. It was not just about my eating disorder and fascination with the suffering of the Jews in the Holocaust. My bleed on the brain when I was born has more to do with me being bludgeoned to death in my past life. Then suddenly, out of the blue, I had a date.

November 26th 1943.

This was the day I was murdered in Auschwitz.

I was 18 years old in that life when it was ended so cruelly.

Marianne looked at me in astonishment. "There is a documentary about the Holocaust on the television later this evening. If you wish to stay for dinner, we can watch it, she invited me.

The documentary was very enlightening. As the cameras showed Auschwitz as it is today, I told both Roger and Marianne where everything was. "The gas chambers were there… the shops were there… and so on, telling them exactly where the buildings were. The commentator was also telling the viewer where the buildings were situated.

My description was exactly as the historian described it!

Many years later, I met a lady who told me she was in Auschwitz.

Chapter 20

Moose hall revisited

I suppose, in one way, my Spiritual Journey really took off at Moose Hall.

Exmouth, a little seaside town in East Devon, with its variety of shops and a two-mile Sandy beach, a little harbour where ships which often waited in the English Channel, to offload their goods. Across the bay was another seaside town, Dawlish, which was always buzzing with tourists, but Exmouth seemed to have a life of its own. Holidaymakers would travel further down to South Devon for their holidays, missing Exmouth. On the Eastern edge of town was a huge holiday campsite, Sandy Bay. There were local bed and breakfast places to stay if one wished to have a quiet time.

Moose Hall, a spiritual church in the middle of town, on the Exeter Road.

It was the first Spiritualist church I had ever been in. Although I had known of other churches where mediums would give messages from past loved ones, I had never thought about visiting one. I still have no idea why to this day! There I was, sitting in Moose Hall, week after week, listening to the mediums and sometimes knowing what they were going to say.

I loved Exmouth, and in the years I spent there, I learned so many skills. I became a swimming teacher and diving coach; I taught children from age 7 to swim and dive. I took part in working with local schools to teach cycle awareness. I remembered the reading all those years ago when a medium told me I would move across a bridge and be a teacher. I scoffed at that one, as knowing I did not excel in school, I had no chance of teaching. However, here I was "teaching" not in a classroom but as a vocational teacher.

My parents still lived in Exmouth, and though I eventually moved away, I loved coming down to visit them and my friends, too.

On one occasion, Jean, Trish's sister, invited me to come down to Exmouth and go to Moose Hall with her. "If you come and stay with me, you can do some readings," she told me as we spoke on the telephone.

So shortly after, I found myself back in Exmouth and staying over with Jean. We spent a lovely afternoon and then got ready to walk the short distance; Jean lived about a 5-minute walk from the hall.

"The medium is a really lovely lady," Jean told me as we walked to the hall. "Have you seen her? Her name is Rosemary; she has been here a few times."

"I do not think I have seen her before" I replied.

The next moment, Josie and Sofia spoke to me, and I saw a vision.

A lady with strawberry-coloured wavy hair, wearing a lavender cardigan with a multi-coloured scarf, was walking up the middle of the hall. #she was about 5'6" tall, had an average build, and had a book in her hand.

Josie grabbed my hand. "Tell Jean what you have just been shown." She instructed me.

I passed on the message Josie had told me. Jean stopped and stared at me. "You must have seen her before, as you have described her very well," I told her I had not.

As we approached the hall, Josie spoke again. "As you go in, there will be only two seats in the front left and three seats near the back of the hall, next to Jackie. You will choose to sit by Jackie."

Once again, I passed this on to Jean.

"How do you get all this information?" she smiled as we approached the door. A lady was there taking the money. "Busy here this evening, Jean. You can sit at the front, where there are two seats, or on the right, next to Jackie, three rows in." Just as I was told, I thought. We sat next to Jackie.

I had been on many workshops with Jackie, who was also a good medium. Often, we would support each other, sitting together at meetings. It was so nice to see her again after such a long time. Jackie was very petite and had long red hair, always smiling, and I loved her grated voice.

After a few minutes, a hush fell over the audience, and the medium walked in. I was flabbergasted, and so was Jean, who was sitting on my right at the edge of the row of seats and Jackie on my right. Rosemary was wearing the exact clothes I saw in my vision. Jackie nudged me and whispered. "This lady is very good."

It was a great evening, and the lady gave a good speech before she began to work. Her messages were amazing, and I know Josie and Sofia were impressed. They were constantly whispering in my ear.

"Tell Jean she is going to come to her, start to give her a message, then move away to the lady in the row opposite."

I managed to get Jean's attention; she was so entranced by this medium that I had to nudge her to get her to listen to me. When I told her this, she sniggered. I told Jackie, too. I know by Jean's reaction she was not sure if she could believe me or not.

Three minutes late, after finishing a message, Rosemary looked around the room. I liked the lady. She was very fast, accurate, and knew where she was going. I could see her guides behind her; they looked at me and smiled. "I think I am with you>" she spoke to Jean. "There is a man around you." Jean smiled, nodding her head. I knew it may be her late husband, Barry, who had passed not too long ago. The medium took a long, deep breath and then looked at another lady who was sitting in the opposite row. "Sorry, I am not with you," she went on, "I am going to this lady." Pointing to the one sitting nearby.

Jean and I looked at each other. "You were right." She whispered. Jackie was staring at me, trying not to laugh, as she always giggled.

The medium was going around the room. Some cried as she gave out heartwarming facts about those who had passed on.

Josie and Sofia both spoke to me. "The medium is going to finish very soon. She is going to say these words. I feel like a steam train; I have run out of puff, so I'm going to stop now."

Once again, I told both Jean and Jackie what I had been told by my angels. Jackie grinned. Jean was sitting here looking a bit glum. I guess it was hard not being given a message and seeing the medium come to you and change her mind. I felt sorry for her.

"I feel like a steam train. I have run out of puff, so I am going to stop now." Rosemary sat down, and everyone clapped. I sat there stunned. She had actually said the words that my Angels had given me! Jackie and Jean both nudged me. I do not know who was more shocked at what I had experienced, them or me.

Outside, I bid farewell to Jackie. I never saw her again. I often wonder how she is, if she is working for Spirit.

Jean and I sauntered back to her home. "I am still not sure how you saw the medium before you met her. The clothes you described were exactly what she wore. How she came to me to give me a message, which I hoped was from Barry, then move on to another lady, and finally telling us how she was going to finish up." I could feel Jean's anguish.

The dogs were barking their welcome as we entered her house. My room was upstairs in the loft. We sat down with a cup of tea and some biscuits, the two dogs making a fuss over us. They were two little chihuahuas, jumping up every time we moved, whether to put the cup down or eat a biscuit.

"You are incredible, Stephen, "Jean put her cup down. "You have a fantastic connection with your guides. I wish I could speak to them and hear my guides like you can".

"They are Angels who help me, Jean," I looked across the room, seeing my Angels there. "I can see my Angels," pointing to where they were standing. "They are always with me."

It was getting quite late, so we decided to go to bed.

The loft bedroom was very cosy, and the bed itself was soft and warm. I snuggled up in the duvet and soon was fast asleep. It had been a long day.

Morning arrived with the sun shining out of a cloudless sky. Jean had toast and tea brewing as I arrived in the kitchen. We both sat at the table. Jean began where we both left off the night before. "I miss Barry. He was everything to me, and I know he is okay up there, but I still miss seeing him. Rosemary is a really lovely medium, and when she came to me, I felt happy; Barry may have a message for me." She put some marmalade on a fresh slice of toast. "Do you like marmalade? Anyway, you told me she would come to me and then change her mind, so I cannot complain."

I had no answer as I spread marmalade on my toast.

"I do hope he does come through, even if it is just to say hello." Jean was saying thoughtfully.

"I am sure Barry will, one day. When you are not expecting anything, he will pop up and surprise you."

"I really hope so." Jean rose from the table to calm the dogs down, as they had begun barking again

It was a lovely time I spent with Jean. Sadly, that was the last time I saw her, though I did not know this at the time. I met so her sister in Moose Hall who would have an impact on my life, changing it forever. I met Trish, who later would be my mentor. She met her sister, who would become a good friend. My journey was about to change in a way I could not imagine.

I met so many people in Moose Hall who would have an impact on my life, changing it forever. I met Trish, who later would be my mentor. She met her sister, who would become a good friend. My journey was about to change in a way I could not imagine.

My three Angels, Josie, Sofia and Sarah, began to show me visions and give me gifts, which I had no idea what they were for.

"You are going on a new journey," they explained. "We are going to give you gifts which are unique to you and no one else. You will travel to many places in the world, meeting people who are going to remember you.

The visit to Moose Hall was also my last ever visit.

Somehow, I knew this was the end, and there was a new beginning for me.

Josie, who has been with me all my life, was not just an Angel. She is my GUARIAN ANGEL!

Sarah is the one who has protected me all my life in a covert way.

Sofia gave me the visions which have helped me to avoid danger.

As I think about what my Angels have done for me, I often ask myself why?

"We are going to teach you so much, "Josie smiled warmly and took my hand in hers. "We are going to give you………"

You will have to wait and see, as that is another story.

The End.

Printed in Great Britain
by Amazon

29230002R00109